INTEGRATIVE
COUNSELLING
SKILLS
IN
Action

COUNSELLING
· IN ACTION ·

Series editor: Windy Dryden

Counselling in Action is a series of books developed especially for counsellors and students of counselling which provides clear and explicit guidelines for counselling practice. A special feature of the series is the emphasis it places on the *process* of counselling.

Titles include:

Feminist Counselling in Action
Jocelyn Chaplin

Gestalt Counselling in Action
Petrŭska Clarkson

Transcultural Counselling in Action
Patricia d'Ardenne and Aruna Mahtani

Rational-Emotive Counselling in Action
Windy Dryden

Training and Supervision for Counselling in Action
Edited by Windy Dryden and Brian Thorne

Personal Construct Counselling in Action
Fay Fransella and Peggy Dalton

Psychodynamic Counselling in Action
Michael Jacobs

Experiences of Counselling in Action
Edited by Dave Mearns and Windy Dryden

Person-Centred Counselling in Action
Dave Mearns and Brian Thorne

Transactional Analysis Counselling in Action
Ian Stewart

Psychosynthesis Counselling in Action
Diana Whitmore

INTEGRATIVE
COUNSELLING
SKILLS

IN *Action*

SUE CULLEY

SAGE Publications
London • Thousand Oaks • New Delhi

First published 1991
Reprinted 1991, 1992, 1993, 1994, 1996, 1997, 1998

SAGE Publications Ltd
6 Bonhill Street
London EC2A 4PU

SAGE Publications Inc
2455 Teller Road
Thousand Oaks, California 91320

SAGE Publications India Pvt Ltd
32, M-Block Market
Greater Kailash – I
New Delhi 110 048

British Library Cataloguing in Publication Data

Culley, Sue
    Integrative counselling skills in action. – (Counselling
    in action)
    1. Counselling
    I. Title   II. Series
    361.323

    ISBN 0-8039-8276-3
    ISBN 0-8039-8277-1 Pbk

Library of Congress catalog card number 90–062743

Typeset by Photoprint, 9–11 Alexandra Lane, Torquay
Printed in Great Britain by
Redwood Books, Trowbridge, Wiltshire

Contents

Preface   vii

Acknowledgements   ix

1   Overview: Introducing the Integrative
    Skills Model   1

2   The Beginning Stage: Exploration, Contracting
    and Assessment   11

3   The Foundation Skills of Counselling   35

4   The Middle Stage: Reassessment and
    Challenging   61

5   The Ending Stage: Action and Closure   90

6   Case-study   116

References   143

Index   145

Preface

I began this book with enthusiasm, both for the subject and for the task itself. My enthusiasm for counselling and for being as skilled a helper as I can be has, if anything, been increased by the effort put into writing this book. Translating this approach 'into action' has reminded me what a complex, demanding and bewitching activity counselling is. Writing a book on counselling has also been a salutary experience. I have come to realise just what a difficult and, some may argue, impossible task it is to capture on paper the essential quality of counselling. In my imagination, I can visualise the clients I have worked with, enjoyed, valued and missed. In the examples I have given, I am not sure how far I have succeeded in capturing their vibrancy, misery, sense of fun or anger at me for getting it wrong!

However, I need frameworks and models to guide me and I hope what I have written in the subsequent chapters will provide a useful addition to the templates you already use to understand and to guide your counselling work.

Case Material

I want briefly to discuss the examples and the case-study. I have endeavoured to give examples of good practice and used some of my own case material to demonstrate as vividly as I am able the quality of the interactions. Where I have used my own case material, I have disguised the identities of clients to preserve their anonymity as well as to honour the contract of confidentiality which I entered into with them.

Acknowledgements

The model outlined in this book is intended both for counsellors and for those who counsel as part of their wider work role. If it is accessible to you and readable, that is in no small way attributable to the editorial skill of Windy Dryden. In the preface to his book *Transactional Analysis Counselling in Action* in this series, Ian Stewart described Windy as 'a master of motivation'. I can think of no better description. I want to acknowledge Windy as a patient and energetic editor.

Finally my partner, Denis Gahagan, has given me invaluable support and encouragement as well as the benefit of his considerable experience as a counsellor. I dedicate this book to him with love and appreciation.

1 Overview: Introducing the Integrative Skills Model

Counselling is an exciting, difficult and complex activity which does not come naturally to most of us. It is something which we learn to do by theorising, by practice and by reflection. As with most complex operations one way to learn is to break the operation down into component parts. Perhaps you can remember learning to swim. You may recall learning first how to kick your legs, before moving on to synchronising arm and leg movements. Your initial efforts were almost certainly ungainly as you tried to time your breathing with the moments when your face was out of the water. Gradually, you became more skilful; you ceased to think about breathing and what to do with your limbs; you became competent in an 'unthinking' or 'unconscious' way. Your swimming now will be nothing like the component parts. It will have a grace and a fluidity of its own. Just as swimming is more than a collection of bodily movements so, of course, counselling is more than a collection of skills. However, developing competency in counselling may be approached by identifying and practising the basic communication skills, integrating them into a model which enables the whole process to be understood, however long it lasts.

This chapter provides you with an overview of the counselling model described in detail in this book. Before outlining the model, I want to define and discuss the terms I have used. The title 'integrative skills' denotes what I think is the key feature of the model. Essentially, it is skills based, meaning that it has at its core a set of communication skills which each of us needs in order to work effectively with clients. The skills are the basic component parts. I have used the terms 'integrative' to signify that these component parts have been combined according to some rules or guiding principles. The model provides a framework for organising counselling skills into a consistent and meaningful whole.

Essentially it is a model of *process* as distinct from *content*. Content is what clients bring to the interaction – their thoughts, feelings, behaviours and their experiences. Content is the *what* – 'What is this client saying to me both verbally and non-verbally?', and all counsellors certainly need models for understanding and sorting content with their clients. In Chapters 2 and 3 I shall be discussing briefly two frameworks for organising content.

The term 'process' refers to what is happening between you and your clients, and to how you are working together. Understanding process means understanding client and counsellor interactions within a conceptual plan. This plan enables you to see where you are now and to comprehend what has been happening as well as to discern what needs to happen, if the counselling work is to proceed to the desired and agreed conclusion.

Let us now consider the structure of the model.

Stages

The overall framework I have used is one of stages. This is common to many approaches to counselling and therapy (Egan, 1986; Ivey et al., 1987; Nelson-Jones, 1988). The conceptualisation of counselling as a series of stages begins to impose a sense of order on what otherwise might be a random or chaotic activity. I have simply called the stages Beginning, Middle and Ending because all encounters, however long they last, have a beginning, a middle and an end. I am concerned also with what ideally should happen at each stage. In other words, what outcomes are desirable at various points in the counselling process and what strategies and skills will be effective in attaining them. The process elements are the strategies and skills which you use to give purpose and direction to your counselling. The model attempts to integrate skills into sequences; to incorporate skills into strategies and to unify the counselling encounter, whether it lasts for one or a number of sessions, by conceptualising it as a series of stages which build on each other. To this end I have identified aims for each stage, together with strategies and skills appropriate for realising these aims. The model therefore provides you with some rules or guidelines for conducting the counselling work.

Strategies

I use the term strategy to mean a procedure. Counselling is a purposeful activity and you will need to be clear about what you are attempting to do at each stage of the process and to know why you are attempting it. For example, exploration is one of the strategies of the Beginning Stage. You will engage in exploration with clients for several purposes, one of which is to engender a clear and mutual understanding of the meaning and significance to clients of their concerns. Of itself, exploration will not solve or resolve problems.

However, relevant and skilful exploration provides the basis for assisting clients subsequently both to greater self-knowledge and to change.

Skills

By counselling skills, I mean competency or accomplishment in communication, acquired or developed in training. The skills outlined in this model are the basic tools by which you operationalise strategies and fulfil the aims of each stage. For example, paraphrasing is a valuable counselling skill. Its value lies in what it enables counsellors to achieve with clients when they use it. Accurate paraphrasing is a key skill for relationship building and essential to the strategy of exploration.

Let us look now at the model itself.

Beginning Stage

During the Beginning Stage of the counselling process you will primarily be concerned with relationship building and assessment. I have identified the following four aims to guide the work of this stage. The aims are the intended outcomes or what you want to achieve.

Aims
1 *To establish a working relationship.* This is a fundamentally important aim and one, I think, upon which the success or otherwise of the counselling depends. You will need to develop the kind of relationship in which clients are encouraged to work. Unless clients believe that you are trustworthy and accepting of them, they will be unlikely either to ally themselves with you or allow you to know them in anything more than a superficial way.
2 *To clarify and define problems.* It is reasonable to suppose that if you and clients are to work together, both of you should understand what issues and concerns they have. Often clients are unclear about what bothers them or they may have multiple issues to deal with and be uncertain where to start.
3 *To make an assessment.* By this I mean formulating hypotheses about what clients share with you. Two of the assessments you will need to make are whether or not counselling is likely to assist specific clients and whether or not *you* are willing to work with them to help them achieve what they want.
4 *To negotiate a contract.* Counselling is a contractual activity. The contract provides the guidelines for the work and is an explicit

agreement between you and clients. Contracts ensure that counselling is a shared enterprise and not something that is 'done to' clients by an 'expert'. It is a way of both recognising clients' responsibility for themselves and inviting their co-operation.

Strategies

These are the procedures you will use to enable you to fulfil the aims of the Beginning Stage. Let us briefly consider each in turn.

1 *Exploration* involves helping clients to examine and elucidate their concerns. The purpose is clarification and common under-standing between you.
2 *Prioritising and focussing* means deciding in what order clients will tackle their concerns and identifying what is at the heart of the issues they bring.
3 *Communicating core values* is concerned with showing clients that you both accept and understand them. Core values of acceptance and understanding are those attitudes and beliefs essential to developing a helping relationship. Acceptance is valuing clients because they are human, respecting their differ-ence and prizing their uniqueness. Understanding means the ability to see clients' worlds as they see them. These values need to be communicated in the way you respond to clients. This is an important strategy which underpins the whole counselling process.

Foundation skills

These are the vital basic skills upon which the work of both this and subsequent stages in the counselling process depend. They can be used in a variety of combinations or sequences to operationalise each of the strategies.

1 *Attending and listening.* In order to understand clients and communicate your understanding, you will obviously need to listen to them. I use the term 'active listening' to mean listening with purpose and responding in such a way that clients know that they have been both heard and understood.

I have classified the ways in which you might respond verbally to clients into two skill groups, namely *reflective* and *probing*.

2 *Reflective skills.* The distinguishing feature of this group of skills is the identification of clients' core messages and offering them back to them in your own words. Reflective skills are valuable for 'tracking' clients, since they impose minimal direction from the counsellor. Using them enables you to communicate and

check your understanding and to accept what clients are saying. As such they are excellent skills for relationship building and information gathering. The reflective skills are:

(a) *restating* what you believe to be a significant word or phrase which the client has used;

(b) *paraphrasing*, which involves expressing in your own words clients' core messages;

(c) *summarising*, which is offering clients a précis of the information they have given you – not as a list of facts but as an organised overview of important themes or clusters of concerns.

3 *Probing skills.* The source of the probing skills is the counsellor's view or frame of reference. When you ask a question, you will be focussing on what you want to know and not necessarily what clients want to tell you, However, probing *is* a part of counselling. You will need information from clients and at times may want to influence the direction of the exploration. In general, probes are interventions which increase counsellor control and, for that reason, should be used sparingly, particularly in the early stages of counselling.

The probing skills are:

(a) *questioning.* In Chapter 3, I discuss types of questions and comment on how questions might both facilitate and inhibit exploration;

(b) *making statements* is a gentler form of probing. For example, instead of asking a client 'What did she do to upset you?', you might say 'I'm not sure what she did to upset you.' Statements are less intrusive and controlling than questions.

4 *Being concrete* deserves special mention. I think it is an essential skill to develop because of the way it facilitates clarity and understanding. There are two aspects to this skill. First, you will need to listen carefully to what clients are saying and be alert to their generalisations, blurring or fuzziness. It goes without saying that you will not be in a position to invite a more concrete description, if you are unaware of the vagueness in what clients are saying. Second, you need to ensure that you are clear and specific in what you say to clients.

Middle Stage

The Middle Stage focusses on helping clients to reassess their problems and their concerns. Reassessment helps them to gain the new and different perspectives required to set goals and take action.

It is the crux of the counselling process because, without a new and different view of themselves and their concerns, clients are unlikely to change. Let us look at the aims.

Aims

1 *To reassess problems*. Clients will have their own views or perspectives on their concerns. Reassessment involves helping them to see themselves from different and more empowering perspectives.

2 *To maintain the working relationship*. This is an important aim for the whole counselling encounter. Reassessment can be tough for clients. The discoveries they make about themselves and their behaviour are often painful.

3 *To work to the contract*. Contracts may be renegotiated as counselling progresses. However, you will need to keep the contract in mind throughout. It specifies the purpose that you and clients have agreed upon.

Strategies

1 *Communicating core values*. Clients are more likely to receive challenges and the invitation to explore more deeply if they feel safe enough with you and if they trust you.

2 *Challenging* means offering clients a view or perspective which is different from theirs and which stimulates them to reconsider their position or view. Challenging provokes deeper exploration, by which I mean that clients are encouraged to explore what they have hitherto been unaware of or dimly aware of as well as what they may have been avoiding or overlooking. There are specific ways of challenging and each of the following strategies has a specific focus:

   (a) *confrontation* is useful for helping clients to identify the ruses or tricks which they employ and which inhibit change;

   (b) *giving feedback* involves letting clients know how you experience them;

   (c) *giving information* can encourage clients to see themselves differently;

   (d) *giving directives* means openly directing the process. When you tell a client to 'Stay with what you're feeling now', you are directing them to do something. You will usually be directing them to behave in a way that is different for them and which provides a challenge to their current behaviour;

   (e) *counsellor self-disclosure*. This means talking about your own experiences. Used sparingly, it has the effect of freeing clients to explore their own concerns in a more meaningful way;

(f) *immediacy* focusses both on the relationship between you and on what is happening now. Being immediate means offering clients your view of the interaction between you, and encouraging them to reflect on what is happening.

Skills
The foundation skills identified in the Beginning Stage provide the basis for the more complex challenging strategies. You will use them in sequences or combinations to influence clients to look afresh at their concerns.

Ending Stage

The Ending Stage typically has to do with planning for and taking effective action. It also focusses on ending the counselling relationship.

Aims
1 *To decide on appropriate change.* If clients are to make changes, then they will need to know what changes are possible and what particular outcomes they want.
2 *To transfer learning.* What clients learn in counselling about their behaviour and the different options open to them will need to be transferred to their life outside the counselling room, if they are to succeed in coping with their concerns.
3 *To implement change.* Change involves taking some action. Clients may need help to act. For example, talking about expressing anger appropriately is not the same as doing it.
4 *To end the counselling relationship.* The counselling relationship will have involved your clients meeting and sharing with you as well as being supported by you and experiencing your commitment to them. It will have been a very important relationship for most clients. Ending is concerned with recognising the loss of this relationship as well as the fulfilment of a contract.

Strategies
1 *Goal setting.* Goal setting provides a framework and a set of criteria which will enable you both to identify and to assess with clients the outcomes they say they want. It is an adaptable strategy which allows for the integration of different techniques, for example, guided fantasy and role-play.

2 *Action planning.* If clients are to act, then they must choose from all the available options open to them and plan their action.
3 *Evaluating.* Action needs to be evaluated for success. The important question for clients is 'Is this action helping me to cope better with my concerns?'
4 *Ending.* Reviewing the work, helping clients to identify and own the changes they have made, is part of this strategy. Clients may need time and space to work through their feelings of sadness and loss.

Skills
Again, the foundation skills are the communication part of the above strategies.

This model, of course, provides a static picture of what is in essence a complex, fluid and changing process. Counselling, in action, is not a neat, linear operation with a defined structure and discrete stages. It is much more complicated and subtle, with both client and counsellor working in their own unique ways. The model, therefore, simply represents a plan for you. It is neither a description of how clients actually behave nor of what counselling is.

However, conceptualising counselling as a series of stages is an attempt to introduce some stable points into the process. These will be points at which the work begins to change by adopting a different focus. The model provides guidance about not only what to do at each stage but also how and when to do it. Implicit in its structure is the idea that certain things should precede others. For example, goals should precede action, otherwise the action may be mis-directed. Using this model and being aware of your intentions as well as developing your skills by practising so that you communicate what you actually intend to communicate seems to me a responsible way to approach counselling.

In one sense this is a meta-model of counselling, because it can be integrated with other theoretical approaches. Whatever theory you espouse, you will need the strategies and the skills with which to implement that theory. Just as counsellors need theories which attempt both to explain how individuals have developed as they have and to provide models of healthy development, so they need frameworks to understand process. This model conceptualises process and enables you to translate theory into practice.

Its strength is that it provides a clear, sensible and accessible framework for practitioners. However, like any framework, unless it is used sensitively and flexibly, it will tyrannise rather than liberate the users.

To conclude this overview, I want to outline some of the basic assumptions about human nature which underpin this model (Deaux and Wrightsman, 1984).

Basic Assumptions about Human Nature

The way you work with clients and the frameworks you choose are a reflection of your values and assumptions both about others and about counselling. For example, if I repeatedly tell clients what to do, my behaviour could be said to be a reflection of my belief that they are not capable of making their own choices and need an expert – me. However, each of us has principles which guide and inform our practice. Being clear and explicit about beliefs and basic assumptions means that they are available for examination and modification. Here are some of the assumptions:

1 *Individuals are deserving of acceptance and understanding because they are human.* This means that you will make a distinction between the clients themselves and their behaviour. While you will strive to communicate to them that you value them as individuals, it does not mean that you will necessarily value or condone their behaviour.

2 *Individuals are capable of change.* Clients have learned ways of behaving which do not serve them well. They can identify and develop different ways of responding both to their problems and to others. Given a supportive environment where trying out new ideas does not carry the risk of rejection or ridicule, they will be capable of discovering options for more satisfying behaviour.

3 *Individuals create their own meaning.* What seems chaotic or destructive to us may have a sense of order or purpose for clients. They may be involved to varying degrees in the creation of their own misery by the way they interpret, react to and try to make sense of events and experiences. For example, clients who believe they are stupid may set goals which they cannot hope to achieve, interpret success as luck and may not 'hear' any positive feedback. They are interpreting their experiences to fit their views of themselves and their worlds.

4 *Individuals are experts on themselves.* Clients know best how they feel and what they believe and think. They, better than anyone, can tell what the pain and disappointments are like for them, what their fears are and what they most want for

themselves. However, they may need varying amounts of help to do that.

5   *Individuals want to realise their potential.* Clients want to become more self-directing and more self-empowered. They have the potential to discover what is right for them, if they are given the climate in which to make that discovery. They have the capacity to think for themselves and have the resources to deal in more creative ways with their problems and concerns.

6   *The behaviour of individuals is purposeful.* Clients' behaviour, however unhelpful it appears to us, is directed towards some goals. Their behaviour can be understood in terms of the purposes it serves for them.

7   *Individuals will work harder to achieve goals which they have set for themselves.* Individuals are more likely to mobilise their resources and strive for outcomes which they value and want, rather than goals which are imposed. Helping clients to identify the outcomes they both want and value is part of the counselling process.

Let us now turn to the model in detail and begin at the Beginning Stage.

2 The Beginning Stage: Exploration, Contracting and Assessment

---

The Beginning Stage

Aims (the intended outcomes)
- to establish a working relationship
- to clarify and define problems
- to make an assessment
- to negotiate a contract

Strategies
- exploration
- prioritising and focussing
- communicating core values

Foundation skills
- attending
- observing clients
- listening
- reflective skills:
  - reflecting a word or phrase
  - paraphrasing
  - summarising
- probing skills:
  - questioning
  - making statements
- being concrete

This chapter begins with an outline and a discussion of the aims and strategies appropriate to the beginning stage of counselling. The second part is concerned with planning and managing the first session with a new client.

Aims

The Beginning Stage has the following four aims:

1 to establish a working relationship;

2   to clarify and define problems;
3   to make an assessment;
4   to negotiate a contract.

These aims provide a framework for focussing your work and for assessing both process and progress. They are stage specific – that is, they are outcomes more appropriate to the Beginning Stage of counselling than to any other. If you do not address them, it is likely that your counselling will not have a secure enough basis from which to proceed to the other stages.

To establish a working relationship
Counselling is much more than an organised collection of skills and strategies built into stages (Bond, 1989). It is essentially a human activity, characterised by a particular type of relationship between counsellor and client. While a counselling relationship has much in common with other relationships, for example close friendship, it is the specific characteristics of the relationship which in general distinguish counselling from other helping activities.

Let us look briefly at some of the important characteristics and dimensions of this working relationship. According to Tyler (1969) and Gilmore (1973), an effective counselling relationship will be characterised by the two core qualities of acceptance and understanding.

Acceptance   This is akin to what Rogers (1961) called 'unconditional positive regard' and what Egan (1986) referred to as 'respect'. Essentially, acceptance means valuing others because they are human. Clients may experience a variety of emotions at the prospect of discussing what concerns them. For example, they may feel ashamed, fearful or embarrassed. Often they judge themselves harshly and anticipate blame from others. I believe that clients who feel judged or blamed are unlikely to feel secure enough to begin exploring painful issues and concerns. Of course, in order to work effectively with clients, you will need to be continually making judgements and assessments. For example, you will be making judgements about process and deciding when to intervene and when to remain silent. You will also be evaluating the effectiveness of your interventions and making assessments about the issues which clients bring. But at the same time, it is vital that you aim for and work to maintain *a relationship that is free of judgements about clients as worthy or unworthy individuals*. None of us enjoys failure, rejection or labels such as 'stupid' or 'lazy'. While clients are often instrumental in creating some of their own pain, the strategies which they have adopted are probably the most creative ones they have for managing their lives as they experience them. Clients are doing the best they can and, therefore, deserve neither blame nor condemnation.

To accept clients means prizing and celebrating their differences as well as acknowledging their experiences as valid for them. Acceptance is neither a bland nor a resigned attitude which colludes with destructive behaviour or self-defeating beliefs. Rather it is a strong, potent quality that recognises the worth of others and their ability to change. To behave in an accepting way does not preclude pointing out to clients aspects of their actions which may prove unhelpful. Nor does it preclude discussion of the possible consequences associated with certain decisions. Rather it implies receiving and giving credence to what clients bring to counselling; and distinguishing between clients themselves – valuable because they are human – and their behaviour.

Understanding   This means grasping as completely as possible the messages which clients are trying to convey by both their verbal and non-verbal behaviour. Rogers (1951) called this 'empathic understanding' and saw it as essential to a therapeutic relationship. When counselling you will strive to see clients' worlds from their perspective and to be open to their experiences. Because we are all separate, unique beings, it is not possible for us to understand our clients completely and absolutely. No one can experience your life as you experience it. While you may share a history with others – as for example in belonging to the same family or attending the same school – your individual experience of that history will be unique.

Acceptance and understanding are core conditions and important values which you will need to express by both your verbal and non-verbal behaviour. Communicating acceptance and understanding of clients assists in promoting the counselling relationship as a partnership. Clients may neither feel 'equal' nor powerful. On the contrary, they may feel inept, powerless and 'one down'. However, a relationship in which they are accepted, and where they experience genuine interest in them and a willingness to understand their perspective can be powerful in liberating them to become active in the counselling process. If the general aim of counselling is to empower clients, then this needs to be reflected in the way you negotiate the relationship from the outset.

Other important dimensions of the counselling relationship may be conceptualised as follows.

Support/challenge   By support I mean being a source of strength to, standing alongside and not colluding with or rescuing. While supporting clients is important throughout counselling, it may be especially crucial to the early stage when the relationship is fragile. However, if clients are to change, they may need to face those aspects of their behaviour which are inhibiting change. Challenging clients means encouraging them to explore more deeply and gain greater self-understanding. Challenges which are not based on support are likely to be experienced as dismissive or unfeeling. Support without challenge may be unhelpful, because clients are never enabled to shift beyond their own limiting perspectives.

Trust/mistrust   Clients are more likely to share and work with counsellors whom they trust. Trust is generally developed when individuals behave in a consistent way towards one another and show that they both accept and understand them. To create a trusting counselling relationship, therefore, you will need to behave consistently towards clients with regard to such issues as time keeping, confidentiality and personal boundaries. You will continue to show acceptance and understanding of them even when they may be attacking or hating you. They also need to trust that you can stay the course with them and to know that you are not going to buckle under the weight of their disclosure.

Emotional closeness/emotional distance   Clients will both tolerate and need varying degrees of emotional closeness with you. You have to maintain a paradoxical position of knowing their innermost thoughts and feelings, being emotionally close to them and yet remaining distant enough to retain a helpful objective stance. You will endeavour to make emotional contact with them while remaining at an emotional distance which enables you to avoid becoming personally involved. (Brammer et al., 1988).

In one sense, it is misleading to talk of the relationship being established at this stage, because paying heed to the relationship and maintaining it as a viable medium for the counselling work is something to which you will attend throughout the period of contact with the client. A useful analogy is that the work done in the early stage of counselling may be likened to laying down secure foundations for a building. A counselling relationship needs a firm basis upon which to stand and from which to develop.

To clarify and define problems
If you and your clients are to work effectively together, both of you need to know as clearly and as precisely as possible what issues and

concerns you are both addressing. You will seek to establish how they view both themselves and their problems; for example, what they believe and feel as well as what they experience and who else is involved. They also may need to clarify what concerns them. They may be vague and confused and open with the following kind of statements:

> *Client*: I don't understand it, I'm not bad looking and I've got good friends. I want a relationship and yet all the women I meet are married.

or

> *Client*: I keep asking myself what's wrong with me, I've got nothing to be sad about – I shouldn't be miserable, yet I am.

Clients will vary in the amount of help they need to clarify and define their concerns. However, equally some clients will have previously thought through what the issues are for them and be clear about what they want to achieve in counselling, as in the following example:

> *Client*: The problem is my friend Helen. She leans on me. I'm always running around after her and taking care of her and I don't get much support from her in return. I'm sick of bailing her out and I want to stop.

Clarifying and defining, of course, continues throughout the counselling work. Clients' views of themselves and their problems may change as the counselling progresses and they gain new insights and information. You will need to tolerate their confusion and work with them towards greater clarity. That does not mean saying and looking as though you understand when you do not; nor does it mean seeking to package neatly their concerns. Rather it means staying with complexity and ambiguity, being open to new information from them and avoiding premature conclusions based on untested or poorly tested hypotheses. Clarifying and reaching a common, working understanding with clients is an important activity, begun in the Beginning Stage of counselling and forming the basis for subsequent deeper exploration, goal setting and action.

To clarify and define in the Beginning Stage means that both you and your clients work towards a common 'good enough' understanding of what the issues and concerns are. It also means that *you* set about gaining enough information as to how clients see themselves and their concerns in order to make assessments and to facilitate contracting.

To make an assessment
Assessment involves using theoretical frameworks (a) to make

sense of and to organise the information – verbal and non-verbal – which is generated in the sessions; (b) to formulate hypotheses about what is happening and what might happen in future sessions; and (c) to make tentative plans to facilitate the counselling work.

It is not within the scope of this book to discuss the wide variety of frameworks available to counsellors in making their assessments. Several other books in the 'Counselling in Action' series provide such a range. However, I want to mention one framework which is useful in assessing the content of counselling. Gilmore (1973) offers a broad classification which identifies three dimensions to human existence. The dimensions are work, relationships and identity. At each developmental stage in human life, these three dimensions present different developmental tasks.

1 *Work*: this refers to what individuals are *doing* with the time, energy and resources at their disposal. At every stage in life, each one of us faces the task of how to invest our energy to make life safer, more enjoyable and more satisfying. The concept, as Gilmore uses it, encompasses more than work as employment and includes all of the many activities, goals and the ambitions which each of us pursues.

2 *Relationships*: this dimension embraces the complexities of the relationships upon which we depend both for our existence and our sustenance. Relationships are not static, they either grow and develop or become distant and wither. We all *move* in relation to each other in order to give and to receive care (physical and emotional), support, encouragement, stability and continuity. In considering the salient relationship issues for each of our clients, you will be asking yourself the question: whom do they take care of and who cares for them?

3 *Identity*: while each one of us has much in common with others, we must all cope with our separateness and our uniqueness. We are responsible for deciding what is important to us and what is unimportant, for discovering how we make choices, for identifying options and for responding to the demands made upon us. None of us can 'delegate' our existence to another and each one of us is responsible for choosing who we are.

Using this framework does not imply that clients' lives can be or should be efficiently packaged into three convenient bundles. Rather it provides a way both of identifying the strands which are present in all our lives and of finding a focus for the counselling work. It will enable you to answer the questions 'In what way is it useful to the client to discuss what we are discussing now?' and 'Are there other issues on which the client might usefully focus?'

Some of the assessment questions you might ask yourself about your clients are:

- Is this client likely to be able to make use of counselling or would some other help be appropriate – for example, psychiatric intervention?
- What do I know about how the client invests his time and energy (*work*), the support and challenge he gets from and gives to others (*relationships*) and how he sees himself (*identity*)?
- Is the client talking about what she wants to talk about?
- What issues do I think the client is avoiding, or seeing as less important, or overlooking?
- Can I discern any patterns or themes?
- What do I know about what this client thinks and feels and how she behaves and what do I not know?
- What incongruities can I discern in the client's behaviour; for example, does she look and sound angry and yet say quite clearly that she is not?
- What support systems does this client have and who offers her a challenge?
- What is 'fact' or observable data – that is, what does the client actually say and do here, and what hypotheses can I generate to explain these data?
- What does the client believe about herself, others and life?
- What constraints does the client have and what resources and deficits?

You will also be assessing process and asking yourself:

- Is the timing of my interventions appropriate; for example, am I too eager to jump in or, conversely, does this client need to hear more from me?
- Is the pace appropriate; too fast or too slow?
- In what ways am I helping and/or hindering this client?

Finally, assessment means looking at ourselves as one partner in the process and asking ourselves whether there are issues in our own lives which are impeding our work with certain clients. If there are, these issues need to be explored in supervision or personal counselling.

To negotiate a contract
Counselling is a contractual activity. A contract is a negotiated agreement between you and clients. I see it as a two-stage process.
The contract to counsel means an initial explicit agreement between parties that counselling is being offered and not, for

example, friendship, a sexual relationship, advice or practical action. Making a contract to counsel means that individuals will know what is involved for them as clients. (See the British Association for Counselling Code of Ethics.)

The counselling contract spells out clearly what will happen in the counselling work, in terms of what clients want to achieve and what you are prepared to offer. Counselling contracts are typically made when desired outcomes have been sufficiently clarified; and they generally entail some ordering of priorities. Clients often have multiple issues to deal with or problems with many facets. Contracts, therefore, are important in establishing foci for the work and are discussed further on pages 30–3. Suffice it to say here that they provide criteria by which both to assess what is happening in the counselling as the work progresses and to determine when the counselling work is completed.

Strategies

There are three major strategies which are instrumental in realising the aims or intended outcomes of the Beginning Stage. They are:

1 exploration;
2 prioritising and focussing;
3 communicating core values.

These strategies are the procedures which you will use to form a counselling relationship, to clarify and reach a common understanding of clients' concerns, to begin to make assessments and to negotiate a contract. In other words, these strategies have clear and well defined purposes.

Exploration
Exploration means helping clients to articulate their concerns. Essentially, it is an enabling and a clarificatory procedure through which they discover what is important for them, examine their own behaviour and find meaning in their feelings. It also involves helping them in the often painful process of sharing their experiences, hopes and feelings. As counsellor, you will be responsible for facilitating exploration with them and will need both to appraise and to monitor the process. There will be tensions, of course, between giving them the space to say what is important for them and ensuring that you have the information you want both to understand and to assess. You will have to strike a balance between encouraging them to talk freely and keeping a focus to the work.

The following questions will help you to assess the exploration.

How specific is this client being? At the start of a counselling relationship, clients may be vague about what concerns them: for example, they may know they are feeling 'uncomfortable', but be unable to discriminate further; or they may have hunches that some of their behaviour is unhelpful but be unclear as to precisely what it is they are doing. They may also use vague statements to protect themselves from the shame and pain they anticipate when they describe in specific terms what they are doing, feeling and thinking. For example, a client might begin by stating: 'Well, my partner and I don't see eye to eye any more and that's the problem!', when what she means is: 'Our sexual relationship is unsatisfactory. We don't spend much time together and I'm thinking of leaving him.'

An important aspect of exploration, therefore, will be to encourage clients to be specific about their thoughts, feelings and behaviours. Obviously, you will need to be sensitive to the clues they give and time your interventions appropriately. It would be persecutory to pick up each vague statement and strive for a full explanation – particularly if a client is hesitant or distressed. However, vagueness is unlikely to lead to clear, purposeful goals and action planning. Helping a client to become more specific promotes clarity and mutual understanding. It means avoiding interchanges like the following:

> *Counsellor*: How are you?
> *Client*: Well! Life could be better.
> *Counsellor*: So, life isn't going too well?
> *Client*: Not really, things are getting me down.

A more concrete invitation might have produced more exploration and more information, for example:

> *Counsellor:* How has your week been?
> *Client:* Well, it could have been better.
> *Counsellor:* What particularly has gone wrong?
> *Client:* Well, work really. It's been a nightmare. I don't see how I can stay in that job and work at that pressure . . .

In the second example, the interchange has more direction; the counsellor's questions are more focussed; and the client responds with further specific information.

Encouraging specificity in itself encourages clients to explore. You are inviting further detail and discovery; and in doing so, you are helping them to clarify their concerns and gain greater self-understanding.

How focussed is this client being? Clients are often confused, unable to understand their feelings and may shift from topic to topic, raising many unresolved issues and hitherto unexpressed resentments. This is not unusual in the early stage of counselling. Some clients may not have talked about their concerns before; may not have had so much space and individual attention nor have felt so miserable. Others may seek to avoid exploring painful issues by frequent switches to different topics. However, you will need to help them focus on the issues they have raised and identify precisely what is to be addressed. I am not talking about rigidity or covertly implying that you know what needs to be talked through – by dismissing or not hearing whole chunks of what clients are bringing – but rather gently reminding them what they said they wished to work on and either helping them to maintain that focus or to find a new focus.

Consider the following example; the client appears harassed and is talking very rapidly:

> *Client*: My life is so crowded. I just don't have time for myself. Everyone is on at me. Even my neighbour says I do too much; that I'm too ready to help. I feel like a pack-horse, loaded up and carrying others – family, friends.
> *Counsellor*: Sounds like you're realising how burdened you are.
> *Client*: Yes. I'm a strong person though and I can cope. My husband feels I should change one of my part-time jobs. He thinks I could get more money somewhere else. That's a decision I need to make.
> *Counsellor*: It does sound like you have many commitments. You were talking a moment ago about your life being crowded and feeling like a 'pack-horse'. I wonder if you've said all you want to say about that or whether you want to discuss changing your job?

Here the counsellor indicates to the client that she has changed her focus and reminds her what she began by saying. Finding and keeping a focus is one way of introducing structure into what is primarily a process of discovery for clients.

How prepared is this client to talk about him/herself?   It is not unusual for clients to want to talk about important others and about what others do to them. They may, for example, have experienced others as untrustworthy, rejecting or hurtful. I am not suggesting that you are the judge who assesses and apportions blame, but if clients are to change the ways in which they act, think and feel, they will need to be clear about what they are doing and how that is unhelpful. They will need to distinguish what they can control from what they cannot; and take responsibility for themselves and their actions. This is not to deny that clients may have very real constraints, such as lack of money, poor housing or lack of qualifications; or that the social/cultural/familial context to which a client belongs should be ignored. Clients do not live in a vacuum and helping them to focus on themselves does not mean discounting the contexts in which they live and work.

In summary, helping clients to explore means helping them to talk about themselves and their concerns in a specific and focussed way, so that they acknowledge their strengths and weaknesses, their achievements and their values and interests. It also means taking stock of relationship resources and deficits, community back-up, and economic and cultural factors.

Prioritising and focussing
Clients may have complicated lives or multiple problems, as the following example illustrates. A client, a single woman in her early thirties, presented a concern about how she related to her parents and her sister. She talked about their unwillingness to see her as the adult woman she was and to acknowledge the changes she had made in her life. She continued by talking about her impending examinations. She revealed that she felt overwhelmed with work and frequently panicked. In her panic, she described her mind as 'going blank'. She was frightened that she would be unable to control her fears in the exams, would misread the questions and fail. She added that success in her exams was not only important to her career, but would enable her also to be in some way the daughter her parents wanted. Her counsellor was aware of the interrelationship between the issues the client presented and how the impending exams might have heightened her awareness of her family relationships. However, in discussion they agreed to focus on exam preparation and techniques and to suspend work on family relationships until the exams were over.

It is not possible for clients to deal with every concern at once and they will often need to prioritise. The following questions provide a check-list which you might share with clients:

1 Which concern is most important?
2 Which concern is causing most distress?
3 Which issue, if tackled, would lead to the greatest positive outcome?
4 Which issues have immediate concern and which might be left?
5 Which could be more easily addressed/resolved by the client and would give him/her a feeling of control and of success?
6 Which concern is appropriate for counselling and which would be best dealt with in some other way?

Prioritising means deciding with clients which of their concerns have precedence over others in order to give a focus for the counselling work.

Communicating core values

Earlier, I described how an effective counselling relationship is characterised by the core values of acceptance and understanding. The purpose of communicating these core values is to facilitate a therapeutic relationship which encourages client involvement. It is not enough to expect clients to know that you accept and understand them. You will need to *demonstrate* and *communicate* these values both verbally – in what you say – and non-verbally – in how you say what you say, and how you orientate yourself towards them.

Finally, the strategies are interdependent and equally important. For example, prioritising without adequate exploration is likely to be ineffective. Exploration is likely to be inhibited, if clients do not feel accepted and understood. The list of strategies is not a menu in the sense that you choose some and avoid others. They all have to be used, if the aims of the Beginning Stage are to be achieved. Nonetheless, relative use may be made of them with different clients and in different sessions. For example, a client who has thought out clearly what the problem is may need less time exploring and more on prioritising. A returning client may have a legacy of trust in you and hence you may focus less on relationship building.

In the next chapter, I discuss the skills essential for implementing these strategies and fulfilling the aims of the Beginning Stage. Before doing so, however, let us look in some detail at the first session with a new client.

The First Session

In this section, I discuss the first session with a new client and propose a framework to guide practice.

Hopes and expectations

While the counselling relationship will begin when client and counsellor either speak or meet face to face for the first time, nonetheless, prior to this initial contact, in the minds of prospective clients you may have been given a form and a personality. They may imagine themselves in relationship with you and have fantasies about you as an individual. Clients also bring a plethora of hopes and expectations to the counselling process (Mearns and Dryden, 1989; Oldfield, 1983). They may, for example, hope for a quick solution, some advice or the 'right' answer. They may believe that you are the only person who can help them or that no one can help them. Of course, clients also experience feelings of relief and a renewal of hope and energy at the prospect of sharing their concerns. For a further discussion see Storr (1980).

To acknowledge this is not to denigrate clients but rather to highlight the fact that even the seemingly most robust and successful clients may harbour powerful beliefs about what may happen to them when they begin to reveal what they see as their failures. It is not easy being a client (Dinnage, 1988), and your awareness of and alertness to clients' hopes, expectations and fantasies will enable you to provide the opportunities for them to be articulated, explored and used. They may provide valuable access to understanding both your clients' processes and how they construe their concerns.

Nor are we as counsellors immune to pre-meeting expectations and anxieties. We imagine what clients will be like and what it will be like to work with them. Our fantasies might begin with a voice on the telephone ('sounds upper class'); or might be fuelled by inept remarks made on referral, for example, 'I've got a really slippery one for you. Should be interesting for you trying to pin him down'; or written in notes, for example, 'has violent thoughts'. You will need to be aware of *your* own fantasies, feelings and expectations. Failure to separate what belongs to you, that is your ideas and fantasies, from what belongs to the client may well inhibit your listening, understanding and assessment.

Making contact
You may have some contact with clients prior to your first meeting. If you have the opportunity to talk over the telephone, you will be listening not only to what they say but the ways in which they are speaking; for example, are they hesitant or tearful? You will endeavour both to establish what they want from you and to communicate to them that you are an empathic, accepting listener.

The following is a check-list of questions to ask new clients prior to the first session:

1   Who referred them and for what reason?
2   What issues do they want to address?
3   Are they 'in crisis' – if so, what is the crisis?
4   Who else have they seen? – if it is a doctor/psychiatrist, you may want to gain permission to seek information.
5   If you cannot see them, would they like you to refer them on?
6   Is there anything they would like to check with you?

You will also want to establish the first session as an 'assessment' session, by which I mean a time when both of you can assess whether or not to work together. The negotiation starts with the first conversation.

Introduction

It would be more accurate to talk of an introductory phase, because the introduction encompasses more than just the initial remarks you and the client make (Hobson, 1985). Your purposes during this phase will be as follows:

1 *Acknowledging who the client is* – in other words, to check that you are *both* seeing whom you think you are seeing.

2 *Acknowledging any previous contact or information*, for example:

> *Counsellor*: I have some notes of your meeting with . . . and I have read them. However, I would find it helpful in getting to know you, if you could tell me how you see your concerns;

> or

> *Counsellor*: When we talked briefly on the telephone, you said you were concerned about . . . Perhaps you could tell me how you see the problem.

3 *Establishing a pattern (Rowan, 1983)*. Clients may both expect and want you to take control for a variety of reasons. For example, they may believe that they are helpless; or they may be scared of 'taking the plunge' and revealing painful experiences. You will want to enable them to explore their concerns in such a way that the pattern is established of them doing most of the talking and sharing in the responsibility for the work. Telling, advising and asking too many questions are some of the ways in which you might impose your own agenda and invite compliance.

The following introduction is likely to convey to the client that the session will be conducted on a 'question and answer' basis:

> *Counsellor*: The doctor said he can't find anything physically wrong with you, is that right? You have anxiety attacks and can't sleep – tell me, what are these attacks like and when do they occur?

A counsellor seeking a more open introduction which offers the client a focus together with an opportunity to start where he wishes might say something like:

> *Counsellor*: My understanding is that your doctor suggested we discuss counselling. The issue, as he saw it, was your anxiety attacks and disrupted sleep pattern. We could begin with that or perhaps you have other things on your mind?

In the last example, the counsellor began by sharing her perspective and asking fewer questions.

4 *Assuring clients of your availability by mentioning time* – for example, 'We have a clear 50 minutes together'.
5 *Giving some information about how you work* – for example, whether you will take notes or want to tape sessions.

The following are some possible introductory remarks.

- 'I wonder what was on your mind as you came here today?'
- 'Will you tell me what the problem is as you see it?'
- 'What information would you like from me that would help you to begin?'
- 'In your imagination what did you hope would happen here today?'
- 'How did you decide to get some counselling for yourself?'
- 'I imagine you have some thoughts and expectations and I wonder what they are?'

Let us turn now to some of the concerns a new client might express.

What is expected of them?   Many people have never been clients in counselling before and may not know how or where to start. It is generally unhelpful to say 'Start where you like . . .' or 'Start where you feel comfortable', because clients may not feel comfortable.

To a client who says something like: 'I don't know what to do here, perhaps you could ask me some questions', you might respond in any one of several ways:

- 'I wonder how you imagined you would start?' (*statement*)
- 'What questions would you like me to ask you?' (*open question*)
- 'It's difficult for you to begin now that you're here.' (*paraphrase*)
- 'You mentioned you wanted to talk about . . . perhaps you could begin with that?' (*summary plus a statement*)
- 'Tell me what concerns you most at present.' (*give a directive*)

I think it is essential to take some time with clients to reach a clear, mutual understanding of your respective expectations. The tension is between answering their requests for information, avoiding talking too much yourself and ensuring that the focus returns to them. You will need to respond to their questions in such a way that they remain involved and encouraged to explore. You may also want to state explicitly that any decisions made, goals set or action taken will be theirs; that you will be helping them and not deciding for them or acting on their behalf.

How you work   Clients may want to know what theories you espouse or what techniques and strategies you use. They may also have genuinely-held but misguided ideas about particular approaches which concern them. You will need to be able to discuss clearly, concisely and without recourse to jargon which approach you favour. You might say something like . . .

> I'll be listening hard to your concerns and encouraging you to explore them. As we get to know each other better, I'll share any thoughts I have about areas it might be helpful for us to explore, or about any patterns/themes which I see emerging. I believe that by talking your concerns through and seeing them from different angles you'll discover ways of managing them more resourcefully or resolving them.

rather than . . .

> Well, basically I have humanistic/existential orientations, although not totally so, I borrow from cognitive/behavioural approaches if need be. I work with clients towards increasing their proactivity and intentionality. In the early stages, I'll be empathising with you and later on I'll be confronting any distortions I pick up. I'll be interested in facilitating goal-directed behaviour.

While the latter may be accurate, it does not convey what might happen in a session. It is confusing rather than clarificatory. The technical language may be meaningless to most clients and make you sound like a text-book.

The working model of moving from assessment through re-assessment to action is one which some clients may not share. They may have different notions of counselling to you. This model has certain values attached to it and clients may not be in tune with these values. Their life experiences or cultural backgrounds may not have included much in the way of being able to choose or of meeting their own needs. This is not to label those who show reluctance to become involved in the process recalcitrant or obstinate, but to recognise that we and our clients may come to counselling from very different starting points. You may need to share various aspects of the counselling model that you use with clients and to be clear about the values which you espouse. Some clients may decide that what you have to offer is not what they want and that they would be better served elsewhere, for example by a different counsellor or by joining a support group.

Will they be judged?   Clients sometimes fear judgement. This may be part of the problem. They may have been judged and 'found wanting' all their lives and consequently judge themselves harshly. You might say something like:

I'm not here to judge you right or wrong, worthy or unworthy. I'm willing to work with you to help you resolve your concerns. That may mean I'll be asking you to look at whatever you're doing that I think is unproductive. I'm interested in helping you to get what you want.

Here the counsellor affirms her commitment to working with the client and tentatively states that she will be inviting exploration of possible unhelpful behaviour. However, telling clients at the start of counselling that you are not judging *them* is usually inadequate. You will need to demonstrate your acceptance and your understanding both verbally and non-verbally throughout the counselling encounter.

The following two short vignettes provide examples of opening phases. In both cases counsellor and client have introduced themselves.

Example 1 The client, Jenny, has been referred by a colleague who had no time available. In her initial telephone call she revealed that she and her partner had recently separated. She sounded very unhappy. She said that she had not consulted her doctor and was not on any medication.

Counsellor: Please sit down [*indicates a chair*].

Jenny: Thank you. [*She looks down at her lap.*]

Counsellor: You said on the telephone that your partner had left recently and you were feeling very unhappy. [*Counsellor tries to remember the client's words and opens with a statement.*]

Jenny: [*hesitantly*] Yes, that's right. Now I'm here it's difficult to know where to begin. So much has happened to me recently. I never thought I'd need counselling.

Counsellor: You've had a lot of painful change. It's hard to find a starting point.

Jenny: Yes, that's right. I imagined it would be easy just saying it, but it's not. I'm not usually so reticent. My life has been turned upside down. Nothing's the same any more and I feel terrible.

Counsellor: Perhaps you could start there, with what's happened in your life and say some more about how you're feeling.

Jenny: [*angrily*] My life has fallen apart – that's how it feels. I get up, I go to work, I come home and go to bed. I feel dried up – aimless. I just wander about the house – I don't have any purpose. He left three months ago and I feel I ought to have snapped out of it by now, but, if anything, I feel worse. I ask myself what went wrong. Sometimes I blame myself and at other times I blame him.

The counsellor's aim was to enable Jenny to begin. She listened both to what Jenny was saying and how she was saying it. Her intention was to show both acceptance and understanding, to set up a pattern where the client did most of the talking and did not rely on her to set an agenda.

Example 2 Phillip had been referred by his GP because he complained of frequent debilitating headaches coupled with high anxiety. The doctor had found nothing physically wrong with him. The counsellor had no prior contact with Phillip and the background information was gained from telephone contact with the GP. Both have introduced themselves.

> *Counsellor*: As I understand it, Dr A suggested we meet. The information he gave me over the 'phone was that you were feeling anxious and experienced frequent bad headaches.
>
> *Phillip*: Yes, he told me I ought to see you. Apparently it's all in the mind [*shrugging his shoulders and looking scornful*].
>
> *Counsellor*: It sounds like you think he's dismissed you. I imagine you feel resentful about that.
>
> *Phillip*: Yes, I know he wants to help; but it's like he's washed his hands of me. 'It's all in the mind' sounds so feeble and pathetic.
>
> *Counsellor*: And you think you're weak and feel pushed aside.
>
> *Phillip*: Yes, I'm too trivial.
>
> *Counsellor*: Your concerns are too trivial. [*The counsellor makes the distinction between Phillip and his behaviour.*]
>
> *Phillip*: Um! And I should be able to control myself. I've always been a worrier, but not to this extent. This anxiety . . . well sometimes it's more like panic . . . comes from nowhere and just hits me. I wonder if I'm going crazy. Do you think I am?
>
> *Counsellor*: From the information Dr A gave me, I don't think you're going crazy. Also, I'd need more evidence than headaches and panic attacks. It sounds like you think you might be and that worries you a great deal. [*Counsellor answers Phillip's question and uses it to encourage further exploration.*]
>
> *Phillip*: Yes it does. I don't know what's happening to me. It's like I can't control myself. I worry about whether I'll panic at work, in meetings. I can't afford to have sleepless nights. I've just got promotion and I want to be successful. I've done well at work so far and it's almost as if this anxiety will stop me – keep me down.

In this opening phase, the counsellor acknowledges Phillip's feeling of resentment at the referral. She thinks that unless he feels free to

---

Check-list

The introductory phase should involve:

1 *establishing a working 'pattern'* – the client talks and you listen. Keep your remarks as brief and specific as possible.
2 *responding to any questions* the client asks as honestly and directly as possible.
3 *beginning to clarify expectations* of what is involved in counselling.
4 *establishing the notion of shared responsibility* for the counselling work.

express his resentment, it may inhibit him from collaborating fully with her. She also answers his question about going crazy as honestly as she can.

Exploration

In the initial session your aim will be to facilitate a 'clear enough', mutual understanding of clients' presenting concerns. By 'presenting concerns' I mean issues which are both uppermost in their minds and which they sometimes offer to test your response before deciding whether to discuss their major concerns. Presenting concerns are real and often painful to talk about. Exploring them is rather like a 'dress rehearsal'. I have used the phrase 'clear enough' to highlight the fact that clarification and reaching a common understanding takes time. Clients may be confused about what concerns them and even if they are clear, it may take some sessions before they trust enough to open up to you. Also, as they begin to explore, they may see new depths to their difficulties or realise that the predicament on which they are focussing now masks different and painful problems.

You will also want to gain some understanding of the wider contexts in which clients' problems occur. By exploring the *wider context* I mean inviting them to focus on related aspects of their lives. For example, if a client tells you of her difficulties with work relationships, you may at some point ask her about relationships in other areas. Shifting the focus from the presenting problem to exploring the wider context is not a licence to be nosy or mount a fact-gathering campaign. We all live in a social context and a problem in one area of a client's life may reverberate in others. The opposite may also be the case. Clients may cope very successfully in all areas of their lives but one – for example, the client who has a successful career, but a dismal record of close personal relationships. Exploring presenting concerns and locating these in the wider context of their lives will assist you in making a working assessment and negotiating a contract.

The following questions will help you to evaluate your exploration with clients:

- What concerns has the client focussed on?
- What important areas have been omitted – not explored?
- What are the implications of these concerns for the client?
- Who else is involved?
- When do these problems typically arise?
- What has the client tried to do about them?
- What support does this client have?

Assessment

Assessment is not restricted either to the first session or the Beginning Stage, but continues throughout the counselling relationship. However, during the first session you will be assessing to what extent counselling will help clients to achieve what they want to achieve. Counselling is expensive in terms of time, effort and usually money. Some other intervention may be more appropriate. You may also be judging how fitting it is for you to work with a particular client. For example, there may be issues in your own life which you think might intrude unhelpfully. If there are, you will need to ensure adequate supervision or offer a referral.

Assessment will also include formulating a tentative counselling plan. Using the framework *Work, Relationships* and *Identity* will help you to decide which areas are of central importance to clients, and on which of these areas you will focus with them.

Once you are clear that you are willing to work with a client, you will move on to agreeing a contract.

Making a contract

A contract is a specific commitment from both counsellor and client to a clearly defined course of action. Let us look at the salient points in that definition.

'*A specific commitment*'   This generally means that the following conditions are clearly spelled out:

1 *Number of sessions*. Sometimes it is useful to contract for a specific number of sessions and then review the work. You might say something like: 'I suggest we contract for six sessions and then review. How does that seem to you?' To a client who asks 'How long will this take?', you might respond similarly by saying 'I'm not sure at this stage. I suggest that we agree on six sessions and then review, with the possibility of further sessions if you want them. However, I'm not sure what you were expecting.'

2 *Frequency of sessions* – the time between sessions should be such that continuity can be maintained.

3 *Timing* – ideally I like to offer clients a regular time in the week to establish a routine. However, this is not always possible.

4 *Length of sessions* – the usual length of a session is 50 minutes to an hour. This provides adequate time for some intensive work but not too long so that both of you become jaded and unable to concentrate. It is important that you are ready to start at the appointed time, even if clients are late.

5   *Payment* – you will need to state clearly what your fee is. Other issues might be whether your fee is negotiable and when you want to be paid, for example weekly or monthly. When discussing payment, you should also tell clients what your arrangement for cancelled sessions will be. For example, you may decide that you will not ask for payment for sessions cancelled with more than one week's notice.

When you agree these arrangements with clients, essentially, you have made a *'contract to counsel'*. This part of the contract is usually attended to in the first session.

'A clearly defined course of action'   This refers to what clients wish to achieve in counselling; what outcomes they want. As I previously stated, one of the purposes of exploration is to help them to decide what they want to change in their lives. This part of the contract may therefore take several sessions to negotiate, because at the outset clients are often unclear about their aims. They may be vague and tell you, for example, that they want to be happier, or less depressed, or less isolated. Your role is to help them to articulate their concerns with the intention of identifying clear outcomes that you can both work towards. You may find it helpful in this context to use *contrasting*.

Contrasting involves asking clients to imagine themselves behaving differently. Consider the following example. The client is talking about her shyness and lack of confidence. She says that she feels embarrassed at social occasions and fears approaching people that she does not know. She reveals that at work she frequently says nothing in meetings, even though she may have a contribution. The counsellor asks her what she wants to achieve in counselling.

> *Client*: I don't want to be so shy, I suppose.
> *Counsellor*: How would you be behaving, if you weren't being shy? [*requests a contrast*].
> *Client*: I don't know. I haven't thought about it like that.
> *Counsellor*: If you imagine yourself behaving differently either at a party or at work, what sort of picture do you have? [*prompts client to imagine a positive contrast*].
> *Client*: Well! I'd be talking easily, feeling relaxed and at ease. I'd know what to say to get a conversation going.

The client is helped to imagine constructive alternatives to replace her current uncomfortable behaviour. If counselling is to help her to change, then both she and the counsellor must know what change she is aiming for. The contrasting behaviour she describes may be used to identify clear outcomes for the work.

Clients may sometimes raise aims which you think are unrealistic, not within your sphere of expertise, or unhelpful. You may wish to reformulate what the client has raised and offer an exploratory contract. Consider the following example:

> *Client*: I'm really worried about my son. He's not working at school. I think he'll fail his exams. I really want some help on how I can make him see sense.
>
> *Counsellor*: You seem very concerned. I would be happy to explore your concerns with you and discuss how you might influence your son. I'm not sure I can help you to make him work and succeed.

The client's aim is unrealistic. We can influence the behaviour of others but generally we have more control over our own behaviour. The counsellor starts with a reformulation and says what she can offer. This is a more positive and accepting opening than a statement which focusses on what the counsellor cannot do.

Between counsellor and client   The contract is not something to keep the client in line. It is a negotiated commitment which sets the boundaries for the work. Since it has been negotiated, it can be re-negotiated. It does not and should not have the effect of being engraved in stone. A word about 'power' – whether we like it or not, clients often see us as powerful and expert. Some clients may need to invest you with power, while others might want to compete with you. You will need to be sensitive to that when contracting with them and communicate your readiness to negotiate rather than impose.

Finally, the contract should cover confidentiality. The boundaries of confidentiality need to be stated clearly and where appropriate negotiated with clients. You will need to be sensitive to the clues (body language, hesitancy, facial expression) that may communicate their desire for further discussion or information about this aspect. A clear general statement on confidentiality might be something like:

> What you say and do here is confidential. However, I want to say something to you which I say to every client. If I think you are in danger of harming yourself or anyone else, I will want to involve others. I will, if possible, discuss this with you first.

More specifically, a student counsellor might say something like:

> What you tell me is entirely between us. I will not pass it on to your tutors. If at any time either you or I feel that you need a different kind of help, then I would like us to discuss it and decide what help might be appropriate.

To summarise, the contract sets the boundaries for the counsell-ing relationship. It helps to ensure that a working relationship is maintained which offers clients space, containment and freedom within clear limits. It also keeps us on the edge of their lives and at a helpful distance.

Check-list – Contracts

1   number of sessions – review
2   frequency of sessions
3   timing – when
4   length – 50 mins to 1 hour
5   payment – when, how much
6   confidentiality
7   goal of counselling work

Closure
Let us look briefly at how you might end the first session by identifying some of the purposes of an ending phase. They include:

– To begin to give clients a positive experience of ending. Some clients may have a history of being and/or feeling dumped. They may fear that what they have revealed is so unpleasant that you will not possibly want to go on working with them.
– To confirm your commitment to clients. Again some are anxious and may feel unworthy of your attention and time. You may do this by summarising the main points of the contract and confirm-ing the date and time of your next meeting.
– To end on a positive note. This is not the same as placating or reassuring which is disrespectful. However, it may mean openly acknowledging the efforts which clients have made by saying something like: 'I have appreciated the way in which you have talked openly about painful concerns here today.'

You may want to manage the ending by doing some or all of the following:

– reminding clients of the time and signalling the ending. For example, you might say 'We have fifteen minutes left and I wondered if there are any other issues you would like to raise briefly?'
– summarising the main points of the session in order to check your understanding.

– making a tentative commitment to begin with a certain issue in the next session.

Endings will be discussed in more detail in Chapter 5.

Check-list – First Session

Making contact
Introduction
Exploration – of presenting and related concerns
Assessment – begin to form a working assessment of clients and their concerns
Contract – what the client wants to achieve
Closure – how to end

---

3 The Foundation Skills of Counselling

This chapter is concerned with skills. I have used the term 'foundation' to describe these skills. By this I mean they are appropriate for accomplishing the work of the Beginning Stage and they form the basis of the more complex strategies which you will use in the subsequent stages of counselling. To describe a skill using the adjectives 'foundation' or 'basic' does not mean that its use is restricted to the beginning of a counselling relationship or that it is a simple skill which has little place in later and perhaps more intense episodes. These skills are essential throughout the counselling relationship and will be used in different combinations or sequences. I begin by discussing *attending* and *listening* and continue with *reflective* and *probing* skills.

Attending

Attending and listening are interrelated skills which complement and affect each other. It is not possible to attend fully to clients without listening to them. Conversely, attending well to them places you in a good position to listen to both their verbal and non-verbal messages (Egan, 1986). I have separated them here for the purpose of analysis and discussion, although the division is an artificial one.

Attending acts as a basis for listening to and observing clients. It is the way in which you communicate to them by your non-verbal behaviour, that you are 'with them', that you are alert to them and interested in what they have to say. The manner in which you attend to them will carry powerful messages, and the effect of what you say to them will be diminished if your non-verbal behaviour is at variance with your verbal message (Argyle, 1988).

Let us look briefly at some of the ways you can attend well to clients.

1 *Posture* – your posture needs to be 'open' and to communicate that you are ready and willing to listen. Find a position that is comfortable, face the client directly, sit upright and relax. Slouching or lolling in your chair is unlikely to communicate alert attention.

2 *Eye contact* – you will be concerned to maintain constant and

direct eye contact. This does not mean fixing clients with a stare, but rather that when they look at you, you will be looking at them. Noticing their patterns of eye contact can provide useful clues as to what they may be thinking and feeling. However, each client is different and the clues gained by observing eye contact must be substantiated by other aspects of client behaviour. Ivey et al. (1987) suggest that if clients are looking and sounding uncomfortable, then averting your gaze temporarily can be helpful in enabling them to continue with sensitive issues.

3   *Facial expression* – how should you look? You will need to be aware of the information that your facial expression might convey. A calm, concerned expression is one aid to helping clients divest themselves of their masks and express what they are feeling. You may want to mirror their facial expression, for example, if they looked pleased when reporting success. However, laughing with them when they describe their hurts and disappointments is collusive and unhelpful.

4   *Seating* – you need to ensure that you are seated at an appropriate distance (3–5 ft) and that the chairs are of an equal height. If you are counselling a couple, ensure that each of you can look at the other with ease. Jacobs (1985) gives some helpful pointers to positioning of chairs. Making 'space' for clients means providing an appropriate physical environment as well as a supportive relationship and uninterrupted time.

Attending well to clients is one way of communicating your acceptance. If your attending behaviour could speak, it should say: 'I am interested in what you have to say. I am ready and willing to give you my attention and I am genuinely concerned to understand how you experience your concerns.'

Before discussing listening skills, I want to say a few words about observing clients.

Observing clients
As I stated in the previous section, attending to clients puts you in a good position to observe them. They too will be communicating non-verbally. The tone of their voice, their gestures and postures will either emphasise or conflict with their verbal messages. Observing clients carefully will help you to understand them. You will learn to interpret the clues and cues which they give. For example, you will discover that, while one client smiles when she is hurt, another narrows her eyes and talks angrily.

Focussing on the incongruities between client's verbal and non-verbal behaviour encourages exploration. They may not be aware either of what they are feeling or the significance of their feelings. Your timing needs to be sensitive and you need to offer your observations in a tentative way rather than telling or informing. Consider the following examples.

> *Client A*: [*in a flat voice, looking round the room and sighing*] Yes, I was pleased when she asked me if she could stay for three months. I get on well with my mother.
> *Counsellor*: I notice a lack of energy in your voice and I wonder what the sigh was saying.
> *Client A*: [*looking embarrassed*] Well, I suppose it was saying I *was* pleased and, this will sound awful, but now she's beginning to get on my nerves, and I wish she'd go.

> *Client B*: [*loudly, talking quickly and in a harsh tone*] I was irritated with him. He shouldn't have spoken to me like that; not in front of other people.
> *Counsellor*: Your voice and tone suggest more than irritation to me. You sound very angry.
> *Client B*: Yes, just talking about it, I can feel the anger rising in me. I was so angry, I just walked off. I couldn't speak.

In both examples, the counsellor specifies what she notices and invites the clients to explore the apparent incongruities between their verbal and non-verbal messages. In the first example, the counsellor focussed on the *confused* message the client was giving, while, in the second, she attempted to help the client experience the *depth* of his feeling.

It is not my intention to imply that certain postures or gestures have certain meanings, but rather that they mean *something*. You will need to observe clients carefully and register any hunches that you have. You will seek evidence from other aspects of their behaviour which either supports or disconfirms your hunches. When you sense that there is enough trust between you, you may want to share your observations. Hunches should be shared in a tentative manner which encourages exploration and subsequent greater self-understanding for them. Observations which are offered as 'facts' may create defence.

Finally, I have somewhat artificially separated non-verbal behaviour into counsellor's and client's. Non-verbal communication is dynamic. You and your clients will be reacting to the clues which pass between you at both a conscious and an unconscious level. Any discussion of their non-verbal behaviour should usefully include a discussion of yours. You may have been inviting the very behaviour from clients about which you are concerned. A simple example will illustrate this point. A trainee interviewer complained to me that he had experienced difficulty in establishing rapport with a client, because she was so anxious and hesitant. A video recording of the interview revealed that, as soon as she started talking, he began to take notes. This had the effect of breaking eye-contact with her. Deprived of cues, she became hesitant and eventually stopped talking.

Let us turn now to listening.

Listening

Listening is a complex and multiple skill. It involves attending to, hearing and understanding the messages which clients are sending both by what they say and by what they do. Your purpose in listening will be to facilitate understanding between you and them and to reach a common agreement about both what concerns them and how they experience their concerns. However, when you are listening to them, you are not a sponge soaking up the information and the messages indiscriminately. The amount of information passing between you will be too great for you to pick up and respond to every cue and clue. Therefore, you will be doing several things: you will be sorting the information and deciding what to respond to; you will be forming hypotheses about what they are saying as well as what they are omitting; and you will be seeking clarification of aspects which are unclear. In other words, you will be listening 'actively'. '*Active listening*' means that you are listening with purpose *and* communicating that you have listened. Ways of responding to clients will be discussed in the next section. However, in order to focus your listening, I want to outline one framework.

A framework for listening

The following framework offers a simple and useful system for classifying the information which clients share with you.

- *Experiences* – what clients experience as happening to them; what others do or fail to do; say or do not say.
- *Behaviour* – how clients act; what they say and do.
- *Feelings* – what they feel about their behaviour and their experiences.
- *Thoughts* – what clients understand about what they do or do not do; what sense they make of their own and others' behaviour; and what beliefs they have about themselves, other people and events in their lives.

This framework will assist you in your analysis of the interview process. For example, you may be aware that your client talks easily about what he does and what he thinks about his own and others' behaviour. He does not express feelings easily or make many feeling statements. You may decide to intervene to encourage him to get in touch with his feelings, in order to help him gain greater self-understanding.

Listening to silences

Communication between you and clients will continue even if one or both of you are silent. Silence can be a potent way of 'speaking volumes' and you will need to listen to their silences as well as their words. By attending carefully in sessions, you will gain some clues about what they might be thinking and feeling when they are silent. For example, you will discern whether they are uneasy, 'stuck', bored, hostile or reflecting. Using that information will help you to decide when and how to intervene. Some counsellors say that they never break a silence and always wait for clients to continue. That seems a sensible strategy. However, too rigidly applied, it may mean that some clients are not helped to proceed. On the other hand, if you are invariably the one who breaks silences, you may want to explore that in supervision. It could be that, by inviting clients to talk, you are making the time more congenial for yourself. Listening to and using silences creatively in counselling means effecting an appropriate balance between (a) enabling clients, (b) providing space for them to reflect and (c) helping them to face their discomfort. The following example illustrates how you might break a silence.

The client who has been exploring a work issue for a couple of minutes in a desultory way stops and gazes out of the window. She begins to look sad and her eyes mist. The silence lasts for a couple of minutes.

Counsellor: I wonder what you are thinking about.
Client: Oh! nothing much!
Counsellor: You look sad and your eyes were becoming misty.
Client: Well! that's odd, because if you want to know, I was thinking about the shopping I was doing before I came here today. I raced around looking for a present for my mother. I found it so difficult to choose something. I've got something but I'm not satisfied with it. I don't think it will be quite right.
Counsellor: So what you eventually chose won't be good enough, is that it?
Client: [*starting to cry*] Yes, whatever I do, however hard I try, I just won't get it right. My efforts won't be good enough. That's how I feel a lot of the time. I'm not good enough.

Here the counsellor broke the silence by inviting the client to say what was on her mind and by giving specific feedback on what she observed. She responded to the client's verbal and non-verbal messages. In doing so, she encouraged her to focus on a fundamental issue to do with her beliefs about her self-worth.

Listening to your reactions

As you listen to clients, you will be thinking, feeling and intuiting. Listening to your own reactions may provide valuable clues both to understanding what is happening in sessions and to understanding clients themselves. For example, you may be aware that you are irritated with a client and begin to pay close attention to what happens between you when you feel irritated. You may at an appropriate time share this and invite exploration. It may be that your response helps her to understand others' reactions to her behaviour and that is how her relationships become distant and dissatisfying. Mearns and Thorne (1988) provide some valuable guidelines for sharing thoughts and feelings with a client.

Listening filters

None of us listens in a completely disinterested way. We all have filters through which information from clients passes. The frameworks we use to organise information from them will inevitably introduce bias by filtering out certain aspects of the interaction. Some of the major hindrances to active listening are:

1 *Culture* – a knowledge of your own and others' culture will certainly assist your listening to and understanding of clients. This is particularly important when working with clients from different cultural backgrounds. However, cultural norms and values are the most difficult to transcend. It may mean that you discuss the possibility of helping them to find counsellors who share their cultural backgrounds or discuss with them how they feel and what they think about working with someone who has a different cultural background. For further discussion see Ivey et al. (1987); and d'Ardenne and Mahtani (1989) in the 'Counselling in Action' series.
2 *Values* – it is important that we be aware of our own values and, in so far as it is possible, that we refrain from imposing them on our clients.
3 *Issues in the counsellor's life* – most of us at some time or another have difficulties in our own lives which preoccupy us and render us less open to others.

Other hindrances to active listening arise from:

- preparing your reply to what the client is saying;
- seeking confirmation for your hypotheses and ignoring information from the client which contradicts them;
- becoming defensive or labelling yourself inadequate when clients attempt to correct you.

Listening attentively, with an awareness of the filters you have and the issues in your own life, is the basis for understanding clients. However, while listening is important, it is not enough. Clients need more. They need you to say something in order to know that they are being heard and understood. Let us now discuss the skills of reflecting and probing as ways of responding verbally to clients.

Reflective Skills

Reflective skills are skills which enable you to communicate your understanding of the client's perspective or frame of reference. This is sometimes referred to as understanding *the internal frame of reference* or how clients view themselves and their concerns. Probing skills, on the other hand, usually express the counsellor's perspective or *external frame of reference* (Nelson-Jones, 1988). When you probe, you will be responding from your frame of reference. You will usually do this when seeking information or wanting to influence the direction of a session.

I consider reflective skills to be the single most useful group of skills in the counsellor's skill repertoire. They are valuable in building trust and for encouraging exploration as well as for discouraging premature focussing. They provide a medium for communicating empathic understanding and acceptance in a way in which the probing skills do not. Using reflective skills will enable you to track clients' thinking and feeling; to check in a non-intrusive way that you have understood; and to impose minimal direction from your frame of reference. The common element in these skills is offering back to clients what they have said using your own words.

The three reflective skills are:

1 restating;
2 paraphrasing; and
3 summarising.

I will discuss each of them in turn.

Restating
Restating involves repeating back to clients either single words or short phrases which they have used. It is an efficient way of prompting further discussion. Consider the following example:

> *Client*: I felt so *punished*.
> *Counsellor*: Punished [*restating*].
> *Client*: Yes, I put thought and effort into that essay and the feedback was so cutting. I felt really down. I thought it deserved a higher mark too. I don't trust my judgement any more.

The counsellor restated a word which was both emphasised and emotionally loaded. It encouraged further response and enabled the counsellor to stay with the client's frame of reference. It provided minimal direction to the client and was not as intrusive as the question. 'What do you mean by punished?'

Restating is also a useful skill for maintaining the focus in a session. For example:

> *Client*: I felt like a fish out of water. I didn't know anyone. That doesn't usually matter. Oh! actually I did know someone but he was so involved with other people . . . Where was I?
> *Counsellor*: Feeling like a fish out of water?
> *Client*: I felt so out of it – so lacking in confidence. I thought 'I'm not as interesting as other people'. Here I go again, putting myself down.

The counsellor's intention here was to remind the client of what she was saying and encourage her to continue.

A caution about overuse   Consider the following example, in which the counsellor only restates the client's words:

> *Client*: I felt so *miserable*.
> *Counsellor*: Miserable.
> *Client*: Yes, and depressed. I wonder if I'll ever feel happy again sometimes.
> *Counsellor*: Happy.
> *Client*: Well, settled in a relationship.

The interview sounds stilted and contrived. Restating provides an economical way of encouraging clients. However, counsellors need a mix of skills. Using one to the exclusion of others is boring, sounds phoney and may well irritate clients.

Paraphrasing

Paraphrasing is the skill of rephrasing what you understand to be the core message of the client's communication. It is letting clients know that you understand their concerns from their points of view (Gilmore and Fraleigh, 1980). The frame of reference for paraphrasing is the client's. Your intentions in using this skill will be:

1   *to check your perception of what clients have said.* Paraphrasing allows both you and clients to know whether or not you are both sharing a common understanding of their problems.

2   *to communicate the core qualities of acceptance and under-*

standing. Paraphrasing is not the same as accepting and understanding clients, in the sense that counselling demands more than the efficient use of the skills outlined in this book. However, developing proficiency in this skill is one way of letting clients know that you are with them, and are concerned to see their point of view. Attending to them well enough to paraphrase accurately puts you in an excellent position both to accept and understand them.

3   *to gain information about how clients see themselves and their concerns*. Paraphrasing is an excellent information-gathering skill because it tells clients that you are following them without imposing a direction. It gives them room to say what is important for them. Of course, you may certainly have occasion to ask them for information and to direct the session at some points; and I will be discussing ways of doing this in the section on the probing skills.

4   *to build a trusting relationship*. Clients often feel ashamed and vulnerable. They may wonder if they can trust you to treat them with seriousness and respect. Paraphrasing is a way of receiving what they bring in a manner free of judgement and evaluation.

To be effective, paraphrasing must, of course, be accurate. You would hardly be communicating good understanding, if most of what you offered a client was incorrect or 'off the mark'. Developing the skill involves both attending well and listening accurately. It also means being open to clients and their experiences and genuinely wishing to understand them.

Paraphrasing is a key skill in achieving the aims of the Beginning Stage of counselling because of the powerful way it allows you to respond in an accepting and non-judgemental way. The following example illustrates the skill in operation.

The client, Lynne, is talking about her home background and how she sees herself.

> *Lynne*: I suppose I've always felt a failure. I didn't go to university like my brother and I'm not in such a high-powered job. Everything he's done has turned out well. He's successful with minimal effort whereas I've had to work hard to get where I am.
>
> *Counsellor*: You're comparing your achievements with your brother's and telling yourself you're a failure.
>
> *Lynne*: Yes! Sort of not quite first class, you know. In my family he's the high flier; I'm just a plodder. Don't get me wrong, I'm pleased with some of the things I've achieved. I've got a flat, a job and a car but . . . [*looking sad*]
>
> *Counsellor*: You sound sad. It's like you're saying 'my achievements aren't good enough'.

Lynne: I don't think they are. I suppose I think I should have done better.

Still it's easy, if you've had everything given to you on a plate, isn't it?

Counsellor: You're angry because, the way you see it, your brother's had it easy.

Lynne: Yes . . . [*bitterly*] I feel angry and put upon. My brother's had everything – support – encouragement. My mother actually said the other day that it's always easier for the second child. That's him. I paved the way, fought the battles.

Counsellor: You're resentful of the help he was given.

The counsellor uses paraphrasing to follow the client and to communicate her understanding. She also encourages the client to express her feelings.

Paraphrasing will also enable you to become closely involved with clients but not get hooked into argument or collusion. It is especially useful for receiving strong feelings or attacks from clients without becoming defensive. Consider the following example:

Client: [*in a furious voice*] It's alright for you. What do you know about failure? You've never been dumped or rejected. All you have to do is sit there and listen. I'm the one who's in the middle of this bloody mess.

Counsellor: You're angry that I'm not able to share what you are going through.

Client: You bet I am! With you, with my ex-husband. Oh! with everything!

Counsellor: And I really don't know what life is like for you.

Client: No! [*slowly and quietly*] I guess no one can really and that's difficult for me.

Finally, paraphrasing is an excellent skill for helping clients to clarify for themselves what they mean. In order for you to understand clients, they also have to understand themselves. For example:

Client: I'm useless! I've been dithering all week. I can't make up my mind whether to take the job or not. Sometimes I think I'd be mad not to take it. At other times, I think it isn't what I want.

Counsellor: You're undecided. Now you've got the job, you're not sure you want it.

Client: [*pausing*] Well! Now I hear you say that, I realise I do want the job. But I'm not sure I ought to take it. I'm scared of not succeeding in it. I don't want to fail.

This client, hearing the counsellor's paraphrase, realised that what she said was not what she meant.

Guidelines for paraphrasing

– be tentative and offer your perception of what the client has said;

- avoid telling, informing or defining for the client;
- be respectful – do not judge, dismiss or use sarcasm;
- use your own words; repeating verbatim is not paraphrasing and may seem like mimicry;
- listen to the depth of feeling expressed by the client and match the level in your response;
- do not add to what the client says, evaluate it or offer interpretations;
- be genuine and do not pretend you understand, if you do not. You might say something like, 'I want to understand. Let me check with you . . .';
- be brief and direct;
- keep your voice tone level. Paraphrasing in a shocked or disbelieving tone of voice is unlikely to communicate acceptance.

Summarising

Summaries are essentially longer paraphrases. Using them enables you to bring together salient aspects of the session in an organised way. The summaries you will be offering in the initial stages of counselling are what Ivey et al. (1987) call 'attending summaries'. These summaries focus on what the client has said and do not include sharing your hypotheses. The most useful attending summaries are those which give some coherence and order to what the client has been saying and provide an overview to the work so far. Let us consider two possible summaries which the counsellor might make in her session with Lynne.

> *Counsellor*: From what you've said so far, you seem to feel resentful and angry about the way in which you were treated unfairly by your parents. You also compare yourself unfavourably with your brother and see your achievements as inferior to his.

> *Counsellor*: You have talked a lot about competition with your brother and how your battles seemed to pave the way forward for him. You are also concerned that you haven't done as well as your parents expected.

In each summary, the counsellor attempts both to review and organise the core content of the session so far.

Summarising is a useful way to:

1 *clarify content and feelings.* Clients often present complicated issues and concerns. Also, clients in distress do not usually organise or package their problems neatly for the counsellor's benefit. You will want to be sure that you have grasped the salient points. You may need to check that you are following the client as accurately as you imagine you are. You might say

something like: 'I'd like to check that I understood you', and then summarise what you think the client has said;

2 *review the work*. Summarising is a way of taking stock, which gives clients opportunities either to correct any misunderstandings, or to add to or reconsider what they have said;

3 *end a session*. In your ending summary, in addition to rounding off the session, you may confirm what the client has agreed to do prior to the next session or what she says she wishes to continue to explore in the subsequent session;

4 *begin a further session*. Summaries are useful for facilitating the opening of a session because they have the effect of bringing you and the client to a common starting point. For example:

> *Counsellor*: I have been thinking about our last session. We talked mainly about how trapped you seem to be, at work, in your relationship. I wonder whether you would like to continue with that theme or are there other issues you would like to focus on today?

Summaries such as these need to be offered tentatively, otherwise you may set the agenda for the session. Using a summary in this way, however, can be helpful in providing a link between sessions;

5 *prioritise and focus*. Clients need varying amounts of help to identify what the salient issues are for them and to order priorities. The frameworks for listening (Chapter 3) and for organising content (Chapter 2) will enable you to 'listen actively' with the purpose of assisting clients to do this. During each stage of counselling, you will be receiving much information from clients; for example, how they see themselves and their concerns and how they view others. You will be forming hypotheses about what they are saying and what they are omitting. You will be identifying patterns and themes as well as the 'maps' which they use to make sense of their worlds;

6 *move the counselling forward*. In order to move forward, you will need to make some judgements about what direction the counselling might take. In a sense, all the skills, appropriately used, will be instrumental in 'moving' the interview along. However, there will be times when you will want to move the counselling forward by introducing a focus to the work. The focus may be for the total counselling encounter, for example, when making a contract, or for a specific session.

I now consider two specific types of summary which are useful for focussing, prioritising and moving the exploration towards making a contract. They are called '*forming a choice point*' and '*gaining a figure–ground perspective*' (Gilmore, 1973). As you will see, in each case the counsellor attempts to paraphrase the client's point of view while organising the information.

Forming a choice point   There will be times in sessions when you will be able to identify themes or clusters of concerns, or different facets to an issue a client is exploring. Given that clients invariably do have multiple concerns and will need to decide in which order they will tackle them, formulating a choice point is a way of helping clients to make that choice. It involves identifying various aspects or themes using an attending summary and asking the client to make a conscious choice about which issue to focus on. Consider the following example:

> *Client*: [*exploring her concerns about work*] I'm really dissatisfied with the way things are. I don't feel stretched. Well, I am stretched in the sense that I have far too much grinding and boring administrative detail to attend to; but not in the sense of developing my potential. When I mentioned this to my boss, she said 'The details have to be got right. They're the most important things.' I feel stuck and ignored by her. I want her to accept what I say. If what I'm doing is *so* important, why aren't I paid more and taken notice of?
>
> *Counsellor*: If I understand correctly, it seems that there are three aspects to your concerns about work: not being stretched and challenged; feeling bored and overloaded with clerical tasks; and not being able to communicate as well as you would like with your boss. Which would be useful for us to focus on?
>
> *Client*: Talking to my boss, I think. If I could get her backing for some of my ideas, then I'd be freed up to do more interesting work. As it is, all my attempts to talk to her end up in stalemate. I don't understand what happens. I leave every conversation with her feeling frustrated, and saying to myself, 'What's the use?'

The counsellor's summary organised the content of the session and identified three aspects to the client's concern. She was tentative and offered the client the choice of where to begin by using an open question. The focus for the work was then agreed.

There may be times when you will want to disagree with clients about which issue to deal with first. You may think that they are avoiding important issues or you may genuinely believe that it would be appropriate to start elsewhere. However, most times the choice will be the clients'.

Gaining a figure–ground perspective   In this type of summary, the counsellor offers her perception of what she thinks is the most prominent issue for the client. It may be something that the client talks about with heightened emotion or returns to repeatedly. The counsellor may also hypothesise that one issue stands out as the 'crux'. If that issue were managed more productively, then the client would have energy available to tackle other concerns. The notion of figure and ground means that, if one aspect of a client's concerns is in the forefront of his or her awareness or thinking, then other aspects provide a backdrop or are in the background. What comes to the fore may vary and change. Sometimes clients are not aware of the emphases that they are placing on certain issues. Consider the following example:

> *Client*: [*talking about feeling stressed*] I feel pulled in so many directions at the moment – very torn. My mother is elderly and has got noticeably frailer over the last couple of years. Last week she fell. She didn't hurt herself badly but was frightened. We all were. I wonder how long she can manage on her own and I think she'd like to come and live with us. My partner doesn't want that and to be honest neither do I. I've just got promotion to a job I've worked hard for and that I'm determined to succeed in. So, that's another pressure. The new job also means more travelling. It's all change and adjustment. Some of it's positive, like the job; some aspects are frightening, like my mother coming to live with us.
>
> *Counsellor*: It seems that of all the changes and new demands you're facing now, the one which you anticipate with most concern is caring for your mother. You sounded anxious when you talked about her. I wonder if that is how it seems to you.
>
> *Client*: Yes, she's really on my mind. I wanted this new job and I know I can cope with the demands it will make. I'd feel more peaceful, if I knew I had some options for looking after Mum and I wasn't so torn.
>
> *Counsellor*: Would that be useful to look at today? To explore your ideas and fears about looking after your mother?

The counsellor used a short summary to offer her understanding of what was the most prominent concern for the client. From there, she began to negotiate a contract for the session.

Other ways you might introduce a figure–ground perspective are:

– 'What seems to be at the heart of the matter is . . .'
– 'What stands out for me is . . .'
– 'One aspect which is becoming clearer to me is . . .'

Remember, it is important to offer your ideas tentatively and to invite clients to comment. They may want to disagree with you and you will need to be willing to explore their different views openly and non-defensively.

In this section, I have reviewed the reflective skills. These skills provide the counsellor with some of the most unintrusive tools for encouraging clients to explore, clarify and focus. It is impossible not to be directive in counselling. What you see as the core concern for a client and what you choose to reflect back, as well as what you leave or disregard, are all ways in which you influence both direction and content. However, in the initial stages of counselling, when you are getting to know clients, you will seek to create space for them to say what they want with minimum imposition of your perspective. The reflective skills will assist you in that purpose.

I now consider the probing skills.

Probing Skills

In this section, the probing skills will be identified and their uses and possible effects considered. Probing, as the term suggests, is invasive and – as a trainee counsellor once remarked – 'We should use these skills with care; we may be going into areas where we haven't been invited.'

Probes declare the counsellor's perception of what is important to address. When using probes, the control over *content* is shifted away from client to counsellor and the counsellor is relatively more directive than when reflecting, paraphrasing or summarising. This is not wrong or inadvisable, if probes are used sensitively and judiciously. However, a counsellor who 'specialises' in probing may invite client passivity or appear interrogative. Nonetheless, probing is important in counselling. There will be occasions when it is appropriate to gain information from clients and encourage them to be specific. You may want to direct them to areas which you think are important to explore further. The probing skills of questioning and making statements will now be considered in some detail.

Questioning
I will first look at types of questions before going on to explore their possible effects and how to ask questions.

Open questions These are useful forms of questions both for eliciting information and encouraging clients' involvement. Open questions demand a fuller response than 'yes/no' answers. They generally begin with 'what', 'where', 'how' and 'who'. For example, to a client who is talking about arguments with her partner, you might ask:

'What usually happens when you argue?'

or

'How do your arguments typically begin?'

or

'When do you usually argue?'

or

'Where do you argue?' (is it at home?, while shopping?)
or
    'Who is usually the first to want to make up?'
    Avoid asking questions that are *too open*. For example, a trainee interviewer was heard to ask a client at the beginning of a session, 'What sort of a person would you say you are?' Questions which are too broad are very difficult to answer. They may put unnecessary pressure on clients to come up with an answer rather than explore.

Hypothetical questions   These are open questions which you can use to focus on what might occur in future. They invite clients to speculate about their own and others' thoughts, feelings and behaviours. The fantasies and fears that they have can be debilitating and prevent them from taking effective action. Not infrequently, they behave as though what they *fantasise* will definitely happen.

Hypothetical questions are useful for helping clients to articulate their fears and explore them in the relative safety of the counselling relationship. Once they put some words to their fears and beliefs, they are available for modification by challenging. Consider the following example, in which the client is complaining of feeling 'put upon' by a friend.

> *Client*: She owes me money from about two months ago and I know I ought to ask her for it, but I just can't.
> *Counsellor*: What do you imagine would happen, if you asked her to repay you? [*hypothetical question*]
> *Client*: Oh! I don't know really. I haven't thought about that. I suppose she might get upset.
> *Counsellor*: And then what would happen? [*hypothetical question*]
> *Client*: She would get angry, tell me that I'm pressurising her and that will be the end of the friendship!

The client begins to identify what she fears and continues to explore how likely it is that her friend will reject her and what that would mean to her. She also talks about her difficulty in coping with anger from people that she is close to.

Hypothetical questions are also valuable for helping clients to visualise positive outcomes and to imagine acting differently. The following provide some examples of hypothetical questions.

–   To a client who is expressing anxiety about refusing requests, you might ask
        'What do you imagine would happen, if you said "No" to her?'
        or

'What do you imagine is the worst thing that could happen,
if you said "No" to her?'
– To a client who seems stuck and says 'I don't know', you might
say something like:
'If you imagined yourself "knowing", what would you say?'
or
'If you did know, what would you be doing?'

In the last example, the client is being asked to construct an
imaginary picture. Exploring that picture may give him some insight
into aspects of his concerns that he is overlooking, anxious about
or avoiding. I shall be returning to hypothetical questions again,
because they can be useful in assisting clients to gain different
perspectives or to re-assess their issues and concerns.

Unhelpful questions   Continuing with types of questions, I now
want to discuss *unhelpful questions*. 'Why', 'closed', 'multiple',
'either/or' and 'leading' are all examples of unhelpful questions.

'Why' questions.   'Why' questions are often disguised as 'How
come?'. They are generally unhelpful because they can entice
clients to ruminate and to search for 'causes' or 'reasons'. Clients
certainly often do want to understand why they behave as they do,
think the thoughts that they have, become depressed or have
unsuccessful relationships. It is also undeniable that counselling
aims to assist them to increase their self-understanding and to gain
some insight into the ways in which they invite others to behave in
certain ways towards them. Nevertheless, clients' understanding is
rarely enhanced by simply asking 'why'. Rather, an exploration of
their thoughts, values, beliefs, behaviours and fears is likely to be
more fruitful in helping them to make sense of themselves and of
how they construe the world.

    Also some clients may not want to understand 'why' or look for
reasons and causes. They may want to gain greater understanding
of their current behaviour, and how that is dysfunctional for them.
They may wish to increase their options, so that they do not repeat
unhelpful patterns. Understanding 'why' does not of itself lead to
action. What clients often lack is the knowledge and the skills
required to act differently. They may need help in planning how to
acquire them.

Closed questions.   These invite clients to answer 'Yes' or 'No'.
They are non-exploratory and can silence the most loquacious
client. A repeated use of closed questions leads to a kind of vicious

circle. The client says less and less and, in order to obtain responses, the counsellor asks more and more closed questions. Consider the following example:

> *Counsellor*: Have you told your wife that you have applied for this job?
> *Client*: Well! [*pause*] No, not yet.
> *Counsellor*: Are you going to?
> *Client*: Yes, eventually.
> *Counsellor*: Do you think she'll object?
> *Client*: Yes, I do.
> *Counsellor*: Is it difficult for you to talk to her?
> *Client*: Yes, I suppose so.

This client faces a barrage of questions. He is neither encouraged to explore nor to expand on what he was saying. The counsellor ploughs on with what concerns her, following her own agenda. The session takes on a checking tone and the client may begin to feel persecuted, or, at the very least, harried. Now imagine the same session conducted using a mix of skills.

> *Counsellor*: Have you told your wife that you have applied for the job? [*closed question*]
> *Client*: Well! [*pause*] No, not yet.
> *Counsellor*: You sound hesitant about telling her. [*paraphrase*]
> *Client*: Yes I am. In fact, I dread telling her. I think she'll be upset and not want to move. There's a tiny bit of me that really hopes that I don't get it, because of the upheaval it will cause. She has carved out a job and a life for herself here which I haven't done, because I'm away from home so much. Our social life has really been built by her.
> *Counsellor*: You're torn, then, between wanting this opportunity and wanting to keep things as they are for your wife. [*paraphrase*]
> *Client*: [*slowly*] That's about it, I suppose.
> *Counsellor*: I'm aware that your voice sounds very flat now. [*statement*]
> *Client*: I feel really resentful and angry all of a sudden. It's like I'm saying how dare she hold me back.
> *Counsellor*: How dare she hold me back! [*restates phrase*]

In this second example, the counsellor uses restating, paraphrasing and statements. The interview is much more exploratory and the client is given the space to become aware of his feelings.

Finally, there are times when you may want to establish certain facts, to clarify a point about which you are unclear or to check information. For example, it would seem foolish to ask a client 'How do you control your depressive tendencies?' if you wanted to establish 'Are you taking any medication for your depression?'

'Either/or' questions.   These are unhelpful variations of generally closed and sometimes leading questions. They are restrictive, because they present clients with two options when there may be

more. You may also 'lead' them, if the options offered for consideration come from *your* frame of reference and do not arise from thorough exploration. Consider this short example:

> *Counsellor*: Will you tell her tomorrow or wait until she asks you?
> *Client*: Neither, I don't think I'll tell her at all.

Multiple questions. This involves asking several questions in one intervention. Multiple questions are uneconomical, because their effect is either to overwhelm or confuse clients. Clients may respond by answering one of the questions or by asking for clarification. In the following example, the counsellor uses multiple questions to respond to her client.

> *Client*: I'm really concerned about my son. He's staying out late, being rude and off-hand and telling me to mind my own business when I ask him where he's been. He's not doing his school work and I'm really worried that he'll drop out of school.
> *Counsellor*: Have you talked to his teachers or his head teacher? Does he have a girl-friend or do you think there's something sinister going on?
> *Client*: No. I don't think so.

The counsellor asked several closed questions. From the client's answer, it was impossible to tell which question she had addressed. The interaction was becoming muddled. The counsellor proceeds by checking:

> *Counsellor*: Are you saying that you don't think he's got a girl-friend?
> *Client*: No. What I meant was that I don't think he's into anything sinister.

The counsellor might have responded initially with a paraphrase and an open question, for example:

> *Counsellor*: You sound very worried about your son. What concerns you most?
> *Client*: I don't think he's into anything sinister like drugs. I suppose I'm worried that he'll leave school, because his exam results will be poor. Also, I'm sick of his boorishness. It's getting me down.

Leading questions. Leading questions communicate to clients, either overtly or covertly, that a certain answer is expected or that there are beliefs, values and feelings that they should hold or experience. Sometimes it is the counsellor's non-verbal clues which push the message 'You shouldn't think or feel like this.'

Consider the following examples:

> *Client*: Sometimes I feel so angry and frustrated when he won't stop crying, that I could scream and shake him.

> *Counsellor*: Are you saying that you feel like harming your son?

The 'message' which the counsellor sends in her response will depend not only on her choice of words but for the most part on the accompanying non-verbal behaviour. Imagine yourself giving this response with a shocked expression and an angry voice tone; and then imagine giving it with a direct gaze, a level voice a concerned tone. In the first instance, you are likely to convey that what the client has said is shocking, unacceptable and that she should not be feeling this way. In the second, you will appear open to the client's fears and feelings and, consequently, more likely to enable her to explore them. I am not suggesting that you ignore potentially serious information from clients, but rather that you do not communicate what you think and feel by leading or insinuation. Let us look at another example:

> *Client*: I don't really know what I want to do after A levels. That's the problem. I'm sick of studying and exams.
> *Counsellor*: Don't you think most people feel like that and end up realising how important further qualifications are?

Here the counsellor is both communicating her own beliefs and generalising. She is 'pushing the idea' that 'this is a passing phase and you shouldn't give up now.' Leading questions do exactly what their label suggests. They control by suggesting a particular direction and by restricting the exploration to what the counsellor deems appropriate.

How to ask questions
– Directly – avoid prevarication or excessive qualification.
– Concisely – be specific and brief.
– Clearly – say clearly what you mean.
– Share your purpose. For example, 'I'd like to be clear. What exactly did happen at work yesterday?'.
– Paraphrase the answer the client gives you to check that you understand.
– Link your question to what the client has said with a statement. For example: You mentioned feeling very hurt. What exactly did you say to her?'

The effects of questions   Questions will have both positive and negative effects, some of which have been mentioned already. Generally, well-timed, clear and open questions will have several *positive effects*. They will:

1   *help clients both to focus and to be specific.*
     For example:

Client: My partner picks holes in everything I do. It gets on my nerves.
Counsellor: You're angry, because everything you do seems wrong. [*paraphrase*]
Client: Well! not everything.
Counsellor: What does she usually criticise you for? [*open question*]

Here the counsellor asks an open question to encourage the client to be specific;

2   *assist information gathering*
In the previous example, the client was asked to specify what she was criticised for. She replies:

Client: Well! usually she criticises me for being broke. I always pay her back, so I can't see what the problem is. My money just goes and I never seem to get to the point of saving any.

The counsellor (and client) will begin to have a clearer understanding of this particular aspect of the client's relationship;

3   *open up an area with a client*
For example, to a client who says she feels depressed and worthless:

Counsellor: What do you say to yourself when you are depressed and sad?
Client: I tell myself that no one will understand me and I'll never feel any different to the way I feel now. Sometimes I tell myself there's no point in living.

Questions are neither wrong or unhelpful in themselves. However, over-use of questions is likely to produce *negative effects*. They are likely to:

1   *increase counsellor control*
Even asking open questions does not necessarily mean that you will 'track' the client. You might still be following your agenda, as the following example illustrates:

Client: My partner picks holes in everything I do.
Counsellor: How long have you been together?
Client: For about two years and I wonder how much more I can take.
Counsellor: What first attracted you to him?
Client: Well I don't know. When I first met him I didn't like him very much. I wish I'd trusted that feeling.

Questioning in this way can invite the client to be passive and set up an expectation that the counsellor will come up with an answer or an explanation (Benjamin, 1974);

2   *close down exploration*
Over-use of questions can lead to a counselling session becoming a question-and-answer session in which little mutual understanding is developed. Clients may not have the opportunity or

encouragement to say what is important to them. They may also withdraw or become apathetic, as they answer questions which may not seem relevant to them. In situations such as this, the counsellor may become preoccupied with what to ask, instead of listening and attending to the client.

Responding to clients' questions
Sometimes, as a way of introducing issues or as a defence against exploration, clients will ask questions of you. They may also want information from you. For example, a potential client who has not previously been involved in counselling may ask you what to expect. You will need first to 'tune in' to what the covert or hidden message in the question might be and ensure that your response facilitates further exploration. You need also to be aware that it can take courage to ask questions and be sensitive to the anxiety which clients may be experiencing. Therefore, it is important that you use these questions. They often provide access to the real concerns of clients. Below are three such questions and some possible meanings and options for responding.

Question 1 'Do you think I'm crazy?'
Based on your understanding of the client, your experience of the client's concerns and the manner in which the question was asked, you may hypothesise that the client is thinking:

- 'Counselling is only for crazy people.'
- 'My mother is a depressive and I think I might be too.'
- 'I feel out of control. I don't understand my moods.'

No doubt you will be able to add more.
   Here are some possible options for responding:

- 'You sound worried that you might be. Will you say some more about that?' [*paraphrase plus a question which invites further exploration*];
- 'I think you are unhappy and confused. I don't think you're crazy' [*statement which gives feedback to client*];
- 'What are you doing or thinking that you would call crazy?' [*open question*].

Question 2 'What do you think I ought to do now?'
   Options for responding include:

- 'What would you like to do?' [*open question*];
- 'I think that's our purpose here, discovering what you might do' [*statement*];

– 'In your imagination, what do you see yourself doing?' [*open question*].

Question 3 [*Client talking about her relationship*] 'Do you think I'm being too demanding, wanting him to make a commitment?'
   Some possible options for responding include:

– 'It sounds as if you think that you might be being pushy, is that it?' [*paraphrase plus a question*];
– 'I'm not sure what sort of commitment you want from him' [*statement*];
– 'What do *you* want from this relationship?' [*open question*];
– 'You and your partner seem to want different things at present' [*paraphrase*].

Questions do not have to be answered directly or immediately. I am not implying that you should avoid either giving information or telling clients what you think. However, in the early stages of counselling, when clients are often at their most vulnerable, they may invest you with 'expert power' and seek advice or even to be told what to do. You will need to acknowledge their questions in such a way that you avoid either implying a course of action or imposing your views. You will be concerned to maintain the relationship as a counselling relationship. How you respond will, of course, depend on the following:

– the answer you think the client wants;
– what has gone on before the session;
– what you think is behind the question;
– the information you think the client needs;
– what you consider a therapeutic response to be.

Making statements
Statements are gentler forms of probes than questions. They are useful alternatives for the occasions when you think questions might be seen as intrusive or inquisitorial by clients. For example, instead of asking 'What does your partner think of the idea?', you might more tentatively say, 'I wonder what your partner thinks of your idea.'
   Like questions, statements are valuable for gaining information, for shifting the focus and for helping clients to be specific. Also, as when questioning, you may usefully preface any statements you make by a paraphrase or summary to acknowledge what clients have said. The following examples show how you might use statements to invite changes of direction in sessions. In each case

the counsellor summarises briefly and invites the client to continue by using a statement. Remember, the primary purpose of exploration is to enable clients to talk concretely about their own thoughts, feelings and behaviours.

Moving the focus from others to self   The client has been talking at some length about her relationship with her husband and his treatment of her and their children.

> *Counsellor*: You have talked a great deal about your husband's behaviour towards you and your children and I have a clear picture of what he says and does. *I wonder how you respond to him.*

Moving from vague to concrete   The client has been talking about an impending reorganisation at work.

> *Counsellor*: You've talked about issues at work and mentioned the various people involved. *I wonder specifically what those issues are.*

Moving from diffuse to focussed   The client has been discussing his relationship and hinting several times at money worries.

> *Counsellor*: We've talked about your wanting to improve your relationship and raised several aspects. You've touched on the issue of money several times and *I wonder if money is a concern for you.*

Moving from content to feelings   This client has been talking about not getting a promotion she wanted. She is showing little emotion.

> *Counsellor*: You have said on several occasions how much you wanted this promotion. *I imagine you have some feelings about not getting it that we haven't explored.*

Statements are an alternative probing skill to questions. They provide a softer way of directing exploration.

Skill sequence for exploration
The skills which have been identified and discussed so far are the foundation skills upon which the beginning and subsequent counselling aims and strategies depend. In order to enable counselling to proceed, you will need to master the basic skills of active listening, reflecting, paraphrasing, questioning and making statements. These skills may then be used in different combinations or sequences both to respond to clients and to enable the counselling to move forward. The succeeding strategies of challenging, goal setting and action planning which I will discuss in Chapters 4 and 5 all require virtuosity in these fundamental skills. It is important that you are able to use the full range of basic skills. It is not sufficient

to be skilled in one and avoid developing your expertise in others. For example, if you are adept at asking clear, open questions, you will need to expand your repertoire to include the reflective skills. You will then have the proficiency required to respond flexibly to clients, to choose interventions which will both enable and stimulate them and allow you to counsel with sensitivity and confidence.

Being Concrete

Finally, I want to discuss the value of being concrete yourself and helping clients to talk concretely about their thoughts, feelings and behaviours. Vagueness does not provide an appropriate basis either for increased self-understanding or goal setting and action. Consider the following example. A client reported that in her family any feelings other than happiness or contentment were labelled 'odd feelings'. She would say 'I'm in an odd mood today' or 'I feel odd.' If this client were to find significance and meaning in her feelings, she must first begin to identify what she does feel. Talking concretely about feelings, in this example, means discriminating and labelling feelings. Similarly clients may describe their thoughts and behaviours in vague terms.

The skill of being concrete involves 'active listening'; that is, listening to clients' verbal and non-verbal communications and being aware of the level of specificity with which clients are talking. You will then be in a position to help clients to describe specifically what they are thinking, feeling and doing. Clients may often feel anxious when they are invited to be more specific about themselves, because vagueness is some protection against both facing and dealing with problems. For example, it may be far less painful and shaming for a client to say 'I don't think much of myself' than 'I'm too fat and unattractive and I think other people think that too.' However, if you were to gain a clear understanding of how this client views herself, you would need to encourage her to be concrete about her current self-evaluation. Also, if you were to challenge this client to reassess her self-image, it seems reasonable that you should understand how she views herself now.

The most direct ways of helping clients to talk concretely are by either requesting or offering a *concrete example*. Let us look at some instances.

– A client has been talking about her lack of confidence and reports that a close friend told her that she 'puts herself down'.

 Counsellor: What would be an example of how you put yourself down? [*open question to request a concrete example*]

The counsellor might also offer a concrete example of issues which they have been discussing:

Counsellor: Is telling yourself that you ask stupid questions an example of how you put yourself down? [*closed question which offers a concrete example*]

The following example shows how a mix of skills might be used to help a client to be more specific. The client is talking about failing to get a new job.

Client: I suppose I was being unrealistic in hoping to get it.
Counsellor: Unrealistic. [*restates a word*]
Client: Yes – they wanted five years experience and I only had three.
Counsellor: So when you applied, you thought your experience might be inadequate. [*paraphrase*]
Client: Yes, I did. But I have other things going for me that I thought might compensate.
Counsellor: What 'other things' did you have? [*open question*]
Client: Good qualifications. Better actually than the person who got it. My rise in the firm has been rapid. I've proved I can learn quickly and take responsibility.

The client is beginning to talk concretely about his thoughts and experiences. If we do not encourage concreteness, we do clients a disservice, because they are unlikely to explore in the explicit and focussed way that is the necessary precursor to action and change.

Summary

This chapter has focussed on skills and on how they might be used to advance the counselling work in the Beginning Stage. I have categorised the responding skills as either reflective or probing.

- The *reflective skills* of *restating, paraphrasing* and *summarising* are important for communicating an understanding of clients' concerns from their perspectives.
- The *probing skills* include *questioning* and *making statements* and are useful both for gaining information and changing the focus in sessions.

In the next chapter, I discuss how clients might be encouraged through challenging to reassess their concerns and gain greater self-understanding, and how both the reflective and probing skills might be used to challenge effectively.

4 The Middle Stage: Reassessment and Challenging

The Middle Stage

Aims (the intended outcomes)
– to reassess problems
– to maintain the working relationship
– to work to the contract

Strategies
– to challenge by:
  – confrontation
  – giving feedback
  – giving information
  – giving directives
  – self-disclosure
  – immediacy

Skills
The foundation skills outlined in Chapter 3 provide the basis for the above complex strategies.

This chapter discusses the aims, strategies and skill sequences appropriate for counselling work as it proceeds beyond the initial stage of problem definition and assessment.

The Middle Stage is concerned primarily with helping clients to see themselves and their concerns in a new and more empowering light. In the Beginning Stage of counselling, you will have been concerned to understand clients' problems from their frame of reference. In this stage, you will be influencing them to adjust their frames of reference and to adopt different views or perspectives. The main strategy which you will use to influence clients is called challenging. It is challenging which stimulates clients to review and to question their current frames of reference and embrace more liberating perspectives.

The work of this stage evolves and develops from the work done in the Beginning Stage. This is because, unless you have a clear understanding, not only of what concerns clients but how they interpret their concerns, you will not be in a position to encourage them to develop new insights. Also, challenging is a powerful strategy which places demands on clients to risk facing aspects of themselves and their concerns which they may be avoiding or overlooking. Effective challenges have their foundation in trusting relationships in which clients know that they are both accepted and understood.

In tandem with strategies, I will be showing how the reflective and probing skills (see Chapter 3) may be used in challenging clients. The skills are the communication part of the strategies, the sensitive use of which determines the effectiveness of the strategy and the successful fulfilment of the aims of this stage. Let us turn now to a discussion of the three aims of the Middle Stage.

Aims

To reassess

I use the term *reassessment* to mean helping clients to gain greater self-understanding and to see their problems from a different and more empowering angle. This entails helping them to put themselves and their concerns in a new light or to take a more objective view. This process has been called '*reframing*' by Watzlawick (1974), '*redefining*' by Reddy (1987) and '*new perspectives*' by Egan (1986). Reassessment is important because without it, clients are likely to stay stuck with the often disabling views they have of themselves, of others and of the world. Gaining the new insights and self-knowledge enables them to see possibilities for change, which is the precursor for goal setting and action. When clients reassess themselves and their problems, what they do is to change the *meaning* their problems have for them and therefore the possible consequences.

Reassessment does not involve disputing the concrete facts. Consider the following brief example. The client Barbara has recently had her fortieth birthday. She tells her counsellor that she feels miserable and depressed. Her voice is full of regret as she recounts how reaching 40 is a landmark for her. She wanted a permanent relationship with children. She believes that not having achieved these goals by the age of 40 means that she never will.

In this example, reassessment does not mean disputing her age or her feelings. Nor does it mean placating or sympathising. In Barbara's case, it might involve helping her to gain a different view of what being 40 means. For example, being 40 does not mean that she will never marry. Many people do marry well beyond that age. Neither does it mean that she cannot have a sexual relationship or that a life without a partner has to be sterile and emotionally barren. It is her view of what being 40 means which is imprisoning her, not the concrete fact of her chronological age.

A methaphor which illustrates this process is the simple one of framing a picture. Different colour borders and different types of frames will enhance different aspects of the picture. Certain colours and hues will either become more prominent or appear more subdued. Some frames will do nothing to enhance the picture and render it drabber and less interesting to our eyes. In all of this the picture itself will not have changed; rather, different aspects of its colour and form will have been intensified and, consequently, we will perceive it differently.

What makes reassessment so effective is that, once we have been faced with alternatives, it is less easy to return to our former view of reality. If we return to the picture metaphor, once we have seen a border and a frame which really suits the print, it is hard to envisage it framed in a different way.

In order to help clients to reassess, you will need both to understand and to take their current views of reality into account. That is the work of the Beginning Stage. Clients *do* understand themselves and their concerns but they understand in particular ways which are often self-defeating and constricting. For example: Pamela complains that she is unappreciated for whatever she does for her husband and family. As she talks, the counsellor forms the view that, what Pamela sees as helping, her family may see as stifling and interfering. Jack sees himself as strong, sociable and 'always willing to debate'. He tries frequently to 'debate' with his counsellor who begins to experience Jack as domineering and argumentative. She realises that she feels verbally battered by him and guesses that his family and friends feel the same.

It can be painful for clients to realise the extent to which they have been the architects of their own misery. It can take courage for them to face squarely what they may have been dimly aware of and yet resolutely overlooking. They need your support in a respectful and trusting relationship as well as your challenge to look afresh. This is why I include the following two aims as important for the Middle Stage of the work.

To maintain the working relationship
The relationship you have developed with clients will be the 'interpersonal power base' from which you influence them to consider and develop different views of their concerns (Strong, 1968). By this, I mean that clients have experience of you in

relationship to them as an accepting, competent, trustworthy practitioner who is demonstrably 'for' them or on their side. It seems reasonable to suppose that they will not listen to or use the perspectives of individuals whom they neither trust nor see as proficient.

Also, reassessment involves exploration at a deeper level than in the early stage of counselling. It may take time for some clients to understand or accept another view as having any validity for them. Maintaining a relationship in which they feel free to question themselves and to explore is therefore essential. Deeper exploration also means that your relationships with them will inevitably become emotionally closer. Being emotionally close and knowing them well may be rewarding for both you and them. However, helping them to adopt a different frame of reference requires that you retain a sufficiently 'objective stance' yourself and maintain the relationship as a counselling relationship.

Finally, when clients are challenged to reassess their position, they generally experience discomfort. Letting go of their habitual ways of viewing themselves and the world and being prepared to change may seem risky for them. Maintaining the relationship as a supportive, understanding partnership is essential to helping them express and tolerate their discomfort and anxiety.

To pursue the work of the contract

Counselling is a contractual relationship and any attempts to encourage clients to reassess their problems should keep the contract in mind as a guide. In other words, you need to ask yourself the question, 'Is what I am doing helping clients towards fulfilling their contracts? At this stage of the counselling, am I helping them to understand their concerns in such a way that they see possibilities for change?'

Let us now consider in some detail what challenging as a counselling strategy involves.

Strategies

I begin with a discussion of the process of challenging, and identify what aspects of clients' behaviour you might challenge. I then provide some guidelines for challenging before reviewing what I consider to be the main strategies for challenging.

Challenging

The Process   To challenge means to question, to dispute, to stimulate and to arouse. Challenging then encourages clients to review and to question their current frames of reference in order to adopt different and more empowering perspectives. The following example illustrates how challenging enables a client to reassess her concerns.

Margaret was a teacher recently appointed to a senior position in a large school. She was energetic and ambitious to go further. However, her new job was going badly. More specifically, she was concerned about the poor working relationship she had formed with an older male colleague. He was a senior member of staff and one with whom she needed to work on close professional terms, if her work in the school was to develop. She complained of his narrow mindedness, obstructive behaviour and boorish manner towards her.

As she talked, it became clear to the counsellor that Margaret was a person who wanted change quickly and who worked with determination to effect it. She believed that her deteriorating relationship with a key colleague would not only reflect badly on her but impede her work still further.

During the first session, the counsellor listened carefully to Margaret's concerns. She appreciated Margaret's vivacity but also experienced her enthusiasm as overwhelming. She was also aware that Margaret adopted a blaming tone and focussed almost exclusively on her colleague's behaviour. The counsellor hypothesised that perhaps her colleague felt overwhelmed and blamed. She also had a hunch that Margaret, in her keenness to implement her ideas, might come across as being dogmatic.

In the second session, Margaret continued with her concerns about work. She expressed her exasperation at her colleague's unwillingness to change.

> *Margaret*: He's absolutely unapproachable and rigid. Things have to change, they can't stay the same. Some of his ideas are so ancient. I feel so frustrated not being able to get on with the job as I want to. It's like being in the dark ages.

The counsellor thought her relationship with Margaret was sound enough to sustain a challenge. She decided to offer Margaret her perception of what she had been saying and to encourage her to focus on her behaviour.

> *Counsellor*: [*tentatively*] I'm not sure whether this will make sense to you. From the short time we've talked together, I've come to see you as powerful and determined; someone who wants to make an impact in her work. I wonder whether your colleague sees your determination and desire for change as threatening. What do you think? [*challenges by offering another view*]

Margaret: [*with surprise*] I'm not a threat. He's had far more experience than I have. Anyway, I'd be willing to work with him, if only he'd stop being so obstructive and nit-picking.

Counsellor: You see him creating all kinds of difficulties for you and you aren't going to change until he does. [*challenges by pointing out the implications of what Margaret is saying*]

Margaret: [*slowly*] Well, I don't know. I've always thought of myself as willing to meet others half-way. I don't want to fight with him. [*pauses*] I hadn't thought of myself as powerful or as a threat. What am I threatening him with?

Counsellor: Any hunches?

Margaret: Um! [*looking embarrassed*] I've been told that I don't suffer fools gladly. Perhaps, that's what I've done, dismissed him as someone who doesn't want to change rather than someone who is scared. I want to get on with the job and maybe I've been too pushy.

The counsellor's challenges enabled Margaret to begin to explore different views of herself as a powerful woman and of her behaviour as dismissive or pushy rather than keen and enthusiastic. She continued by considering the possibility that she had tried to effect too much change too quickly and been hasty in labelling others as obstructive. The counsellor was not concerned to referee or to blame but rather to enable Margaret to look differently at her own and her colleague's behaviour. Exploring a different perspective might help her to reassess the situation and subsequently decide on an approach which would give her a better chance of getting what she wanted.

Challenging does not imply that there is a *right way* of looking at situations or that there is 'a reality' which the counsellor operates within and which the client must be helped to espouse. Rather your intention in challenging will be to facilitate the kind of deeper exploration which prompts clients to reassess themselves and their concerns. Let us look briefly at what deeper exploration means.

Deeper exploration   Deeper exploration has a quality and intensity which exploration in the Beginning Stage does not have. For clients, it carries the potential both of renewed energy as they gain clearer self-understanding and of disquiet as they begin to relinquish 'old' perspectives. The focus of deeper exploration is what clients are either unaware or dimly aware of, as well as what they may be avoiding, ignoring or overlooking. It has been usefully described as helping clients overcome 'blind spots' (Egan, 1986). Deeper exploration is a development of the exploration initiated in the Beginning Stage. This means that it has its roots both in the clear understanding you have gained of clients' views of their concerns and in your understanding based on your different perspective.

In skill terms, it involves listening both to what clients are saying and also to what they are implying, hinting at or not saying. In other words, it is listening for the *unexpressed*, and understanding the possible significance of that for clients. Egan (1986) refers to this as *advanced empathy*, meaning the ability to discern and understand the deeper meanings in what clients are exploring. Essentially, as you gain a deeper understanding of clients and communicate that understanding, so you will influence them to deeper exploration and greater self-understanding (Truax and Carkhuff, 1967).

Deeper understanding and those counsellor responses which demonstrate it are hard to portray in writing, because much of the significant interaction is both subtle and non-verbal; for example, facial expression, voice tone, body posture or a fleeting glance. Accurately reflecting what your client is communicating relies on your ability both to sense and to distil the deeper meaning from the packaging which may surround it. The following provide some ways in which you might facilitate deeper exploration:

1 *Focussing on what clients hint at or imply.* Consider the following example. The client, Josie, is discussing her dissatisfaction with work and says she is considering resigning.

> *Josie*: I really can't see the situation improving. I won't have any trouble getting another job. I'm prepared to do temporary work until I find another permanent job which is suitable. I've been thinking how to answer questions about my reasons for leaving this job too.
> *Counsellor*: You said you were considering resigning – it sounds like you've decided to do that.
> *Josie*: Yes, I have. I realised hearing myself talk about going for interviews that I've stuck this job because I thought I *should* stick it out for a while longer. I haven't given it long enough and I *oughtn't* to leave quite so soon.

The counsellor encouraged deeper exploration by turning Josie's attention to what she had implied. The outcome was that Josie began to voice some of the 'rules' by which she lived her life and which had inhibited her from taking action.

2 *Identifying themes and patterns.* Attending carefully to clients, you may discern patterns or themes which permeate their lives and which provide an explanation for what is going on for them now. Recognising and exploring underlying patterns helps them to gain a sense of coherence where perhaps previously they experienced confusion. Clients may give clues as to the patterns in the lives, for example, by saying something like: 'Here I go again' or 'This is always happening to me.'

Let us consider the following example. Janet is complaining of being used by her friends who expect her to support them. In an earlier session, she told the counsellor that she looked after herself and her younger sister when they were both small, because her mother had always worked outside the home.

Janet: I'm fed up with Ros. She 'phoned me again last night and never even asked how I was. She just went on and on about her problems. I listened and talked things through with her. But she didn't want to listen to me and hear about me. She said, 'It's different for you. You're so capable.' I suppose I am.

Counsellor: You've told me last week how you looked after yourself and your sister. Now you are looking after friends seemingly more than you want to. I'm getting a picture of someone who has done a lot of caring for others in her life. Being a 'caretaker' seems to be a pattern for you, or am I reading too much into what you've said?

The counsellor identifies the theme of being a 'caretaker'. She uses a summary both to acknowledge what Janet has said and to offer her this perspective. She ends by asking the client for her views. Janet goes on to explore the significance of that theme and in doing so gains an increased understanding of herself and her relationships with others.

3   *Making connections*. Clients may fail to make the connections between events which would enable them to gain a deeper understanding of themselves and their concerns. Making connections is rather like completing a jigsaw. The individual pieces have meaning and significance when they are put together which they do not have when they are viewed separately. Let us consider the following example: Nancy, a client, related that she felt exhausted, drained and irritable much of the time. She feared that she was depressed and quoted from a book about depression which she had read. After listening for a while the counsellor responded.

Counsellor: You've told me something about your job and your family, but I'm not sure exactly what your daily routine actually involves.

Nancy: I'm usually in work by 7.00 a.m. so that I can make a start before the others arrive and the meetings begin. I can also leave a bit early, say 5 o'clock, to pick Ben up from the child-minder. I usually give him his tea and play with him until about 7 p.m. when we start the bedtime routine. He's in bed by about 7.30 and then I sometimes get our meal, if John is working late. We eat about 8.30. That's about it.

Counsellor: From your description, I think your exhaustion and irritability have more to do with overwork than depression. I wonder what you were thinking and feeling as you were talking.

Nancy: I was thinking 'How the hell do I manage it all!' I could feel myself drooping as I was telling you. It wasn't until I started to tell you what I did, that I realised how crowded and fraught life is at present. Perhaps you're right. I'm feeling irritable because I'm overtired and overworked, not because I'm depressed.

This client was not making the connection between work and family demands and feeling exhausted and irritable. She continued to explore how seeing herself as a depressed person was preferable to '*merely being tired*'. The latter for her was a sign of weakness.

At its core, deeper exploration implies a shift in focus from the apparent, visible meanings in what clients are saying to the underlying, hidden communication. Let us now consider what aspects of clients' behaviour we might usefully challenge.

What to challenge Essentially you will be challenging the way clients interpret events to make sense of and to fit their view of the world or their 'frames of reference'. Clients' interpretations may be potentially restricting; in other words, they may have 'faulty' maps which they are using to inform their views. The aim of challenging is to enable clients to reassess and gain different, less obstructed views. It is from these different views that they will be able to identify possibilities for constructive change. More specifically, you might challenge when you notice any of the following.

1 *Overlooking of resources and deficits.* Often clients do not have a clear picture of their resources and deficits. As you listen to clients you may 'hear' how they overlook the skills they have or how they brush aside what you hypothesise might be genuine constraints.
2 *Discrepancies.* As you listen and attend to clients you will become aware when things do not 'add up'. I will be discussing how to challenge discrepancies in the later section on Confrontation.
3 *Lack of understanding of the consequences of behaviour.* Clients may be unaware of how their behaviour might affect others. For example, let us consider the following exchange from a session with a client.

Joanne is angry about the way her family both ignore and use her.

Joanne: I don't make many demands on David or the children. I put them first. I always have. Yet they don't seem concerned about what I want. It's always 'Mum will do it' or 'She won't mind'. But I do mind. I mind a lot.
Counsellor: I don't want to sound harsh. Perhaps by taking a back-seat for so long, you've been allowing them to overlook what you want. Does that make any sense to you?

Joanne has overlooked the consequences of her behaviour. By not making demands on her family she has allowed them to take her for granted.

4   *Beliefs and the inferences drawn from those beliefs.* Clients may have irrational beliefs which are both distressing and inhibiting. Ellis (1962) has identified the typical self-defeating beliefs which can disable clients. One such belief is that *'the past determines what I will think and feel today'*. I am not denying the impact of the past, but past events do not have to determine present behaviour. A concrete example is a client who reported that as a child he would worry and goad his father in order to get attention. He behaved similarly with his partner, telling the counsellor, with an air of finality, that he lacked affection as a child and that was why he was like he was now. Clients may be unaware of their beliefs. Their behaviour in counselling and their reports of their actions will give you clues as to what they might be. These beliefs are often expressed as 'shoulds', 'musts' and 'oughts': for example, 'I shouldn't be angry'; 'She had a perfect right to do what she did'; or 'He should be punished for what he did.'

Challenging and subsequent deeper exploration can help clients to become aware of their beliefs and the inferences drawn from them. You may then proceed to help clients restate their beliefs in a less dogmatic way. For a fuller exploration of ways of tackling erroneous and self-defeating beliefs in counselling, see *Cognitive-Behavioural Counselling in Action* by Trower et al. (1988) and *Rational-Emotive Counselling in Action* by Dryden (1990) in the 'Counselling in Action' series. In his book *Effective Thinking Skills*, Nelson-Jones (1989) also provides some excellent examples of the oppressive beliefs which people allow to govern their lives, together with some useful interventions and training exercises.

5   *Unexpressed feelings.* Clients may find it difficult to label and to express their feelings. They may act as though certain feelings are wrong or unhelpful. Sometimes too they will mask one feeling with another; for example, laughing to cover pain. Let us consider the following example which illustrates how new awareness may be facilitated by helping a client identify and express feelings.

The client, Bob, wanted to set boundaries on an ever-increasing demand for his time. He responded to any attempt by his counsellor to focus on feelings with a thought or a belief. The counsellor sensed he was angry and scared of admitting it.

Counsellor: I guess you felt angry at being called out on your day off.
Bob: I don't think it's a matter of being annoyed. It's my job.
Counsellor: I notice that you don't say how you're feeling. Perhaps I've
   got it wrong and you don't have any feelings about losing your day
   off. Perhaps that's OK with you. [*counsellor uses statements to give
   her perspective*]
Bob: You're wrong. Of course I have feelings. When the 'phone rang
   yesterday, I felt very angry. I told myself 'Calm down. Blowing your
   top won't do any good.'

Bob had identified that he was angry. The counsellor prompted
him to explore what significance that feeling had for him. He
began to see that he was allowing others to place unreasonable
work demands on him. He also confronted his rigid beliefs about
work, which were that he should never say 'no' because the
consequences would be rejection by others.

Challenging clients to explore underlying feelings helps them to
begin to view themselves and their problems from different angles.
Let us now consider how to challenge.

How to challenge
1 *Be tentative*. Challenging involves sharing your perspectives and
   hunches. Clients will be more likely to listen to and explore
   alternative views, if they are expressed tentatively. Telling or
   informing may seem dominating and may create defence. Tentativeness does not mean being diffident and endlessly qualifying
   what you are trying to say with 'ifs' and 'buts'. Rather it means
   communicating that what you are saying is open to modification.
   You might communicate tentativeness by saying, for example,
   'I'm wondering if . . .' or 'How does this seem to you . . .?' or
   'My guess is . . .' or 'My hunch is . . .'.
2 *Remember the aims of challenging*. People have become clients
   because they want to change their behaviour, in order to handle
   aspects of their lives more successfully. There may be much that
   they say in sessions, about which you are tempted to encourage
   them to talk more. However, the aim of challenging is to help
   clients to reassess themselves and the concerns they bring, in
   order to set goals and take effective action. You will need to
   monitor whether your challenges are helping them to do that.
   Keeping the aims of challenging in mind is one way of keeping
   your work focussed. Also, the decision about what to challenge
   should be based on the agreed contract and not on the counsellor's inquisitiveness.
3 *Consider whether the client is able to receive the challenge and*

use it. Sometimes clients are raw and vulnerable. They need time to let themselves heal a little before facing aspects of the problem which belong to them. A colleague once remarked 'If your skin is raw, even a small puff of breeze stings.' The most skilled and insightful challenges are not going to further the counselling work, if clients are neither able to hear nor use them. Clients who are in a highly charged emotional state may not be amenable to challenging. Consider the following example.

A distressed pupil was complaining bitterly and furiously about what she considered to be unfair treatment by another teacher. The teacher/counsellor responded by saying, 'From what you've said, it does sound like the joke misfired and you provoked him.' On hearing this, the youngster fled in a rage. She was not willing to look at her behaviour. She was smarting from what she saw as unfair treatment. If the counsellor had listened and accepted her point of view as one that was valid for her and allowed her to express her anger, she might then have been willing to consider what her part was in the episode.

4   *Keep the perspective you are offering close to the message which the client is conveying.* Perspectives which are at wide variance with the message the client is communicating may seem like wild guesses or invitations to engage in extravagant speculation. I like to think of a challenge as an 'obvious revelation'. By that I mean, once clients hear your view, they wonder how they could have overlooked such an obvious perspective which reveals important clues as to how they are behaving as they are. An example of a perspective which might be difficult for a client to use because it is far removed from what she is saying is:

Client: I feel so fed up now that John's gone back to school. The house seems really empty. I'd forgotten how much I miss him.
Counsellor: You told me that your father was away when you were born and during your early childhood. Perhaps your sadness is also to do with the abandonment you felt then.

5   *Be concrete.* Vague challenges are usually unhelpful because they do not state clearly which aspect of clients' thoughts, feelings or behaviour might usefully be explored further. You will need to state precisely and clearly what you notice or think. Consider the following examples.

A client was experiencing low self-esteem. The counsellor noticed that he brushed aside any compliments or positive statements from her. She challenged him in a vague and unhelpful way as follows:

Counsellor: When I've complimented you or said anything positive to you, you've usually brushed it aside. I guess not accepting praise contributes to your low self-esteem. What do you think?

A more concrete challenge might have been something like:

Counsellor: I noticed that when I complimented you on how you tackled your colleague, you said 'Oh, that! Anyone could have done that.' You seemed to dismiss what I said. I wonder if you brush aside the positive comments from others, and then feel undervalued. What do you think?

Here the counsellor commented specifically on the client's behaviour before offering her own view. The intervention gave a much clearer indication of what the client might usefully explore further.

6 *Avoid blaming.* Challenging does not mean apportioning blame. Clients are more likely to use a challenge, if they feel accepted and understood rather than criticised. Recognising and acknowledging unhelpful beliefs and behaviour is not the same as condemning.

7 *Encourage and facilitate self-challenge.* Let us consider the following example. A client, Penny, in her mid-thirties, was talking of a particularly harrowing break-up of her relationship. She focussed on her partner's faults, and on the humiliations and hurt she had suffered. She presented herself as passive and as a victim. Penny ignored invitations to explore her own behaviour. It was not until some weeks later when she said, in a quiet voice, 'I guess Bob and I were really bad for one another', that the counsellor realised that Penny had begun to challenge herself and to reassess her version of past events. She was shifting from a position of 'it's all his fault' to a view of 'perhaps I was also in some way responsible'. The way was then open for the counsellor to encourage Penny to explore how she allowed herself to be oppressed to the point where she became depressed and physically run down.

You can encourage *self-challenge* by accurate paraphrasing and restating. Letting clients hear what they have said often encourages them to reassess their perceptions. Offering the conclusions you have drawn from what they have told you also invites self-challenge. For example, the counsellor might have said to Penny:

Counsellor: You're telling me that you had no option but to stay and tolerate the situation. Is that right?

8 *Be open to challenge yourself.* The ways in which you can be open to challenge yourself are:

(a)   by listening non-defensively when clients point out in what ways you may have been unhelpful;

(b)   by openly sharing with clients when you think the counselling process has been inhibited by collusion or competition and owning your part in that;

(c)   by exploring your own behaviour and challenging yourself.

In other words, do not expect clients to receive your challenges with openness, unless you are prepared to do the same.

9   *Use the challenging sequence* You will recall that in Chapter 2 I introduced the notion of skill sequences. I want to reintroduce this notion and provide some guidelines for using the reflective and the probing skills in challenging. The following example illustrates how skills are used in challenging.

The client, Dave, is someone who sees himself as honest and straightforward in his dealings with others. His counsellor, on the other hand, experiences him rather differently. Her view is that he comes across as critical and negative. Her aim, therefore, is to encourage him to explore his behaviour and view it from a different perspective.

Counsellor: So, saying what you think honestly and directly sounds important for you. [*paraphrase*]

Dave: Yes, it is. I think people expect it . . . and anyway, if they can't take the truth, they shouldn't ask.

Counsellor: When you said 'take the truth', it sounds like you expect honesty to be painful. [*paraphrase to focus on what client was implying*]

Dave: [*with a hollow laugh and avoiding direct comment on the counsellor's paraphrase*] I say what I think, if I'm asked. At work yesterday, I was asked by a colleague what I thought of a report he'd written and I told him straight that I thought it was disappointing. I pointed out where it was too superficial. He didn't like it much, but that was my honest opinion.

Counsellor: Dave, from the way you described the feedback you gave your colleague, it sounded to me like you focussed on what was wrong with his report. I wonder whether he experienced your 'straight talking' and honesty as criticism and was hurt. Does that make any sense to you? [*summarises both to check that she has understood her client and to offer her perspective. She ends with a tentative question to encourage Dave to stay involved in the exploration.*]

Dave: He asked me what I thought of it and I told him.

Counsellor: [*noticing that Dave has ignored her challenge*] And there was nothing good in it. [*uses a statement to focus on what Dave has implied*]

Dave: No! Some parts of it were good. In fact, some bits were excellent, but . . . I was going to say 'That's not being straight or honest' . . . but of course it is.

Counsellor: From what you've said so far, it sounds to me like being honest and direct usually involves you being critical. Is that worth exploring further, do you think?

The skills outlined in Chapter 3 can be used in different combinations and sequences to challenge. It is also important to remember that effective challenges are not developed by simply stringing basic skills together. Your perspectives will be based on careful listening and attention to your clients and will be explainable in terms of whichever counselling theory you espouse. Several other books in the 'Counselling in Action' series provide different theoretical perspectives which you might use to assist your understanding of what clients bring. Of course, supervision also provides an opportunity for exploring how and in what areas to challenge clients.

Some guidelines for using skills to challenge are:

- identify the client's core messages and paraphrase to check and show understanding;
- then add your understanding of the meaning of the client's messages in a short summary or a statement;
- return the focus to the client. When you give a client your perspective or interpretation you temporarily move the focus to yourself. It is important that you end by asking clients for their reactions to what you have offered. You might say something like:
  - 'How does that sound to you?'
  - 'Does that make any sense as a way of looking at what you've said?'
  - 'What do you think about what I've just said?'
  - 'Is that a useful way to look at what you've been saying?'

Types of Challenge

So far in this chapter, I have discussed challenging as a strategy, through which clients are enabled to explore their concerns more deeply in order to arrive at a new and different awareness. I have identified some of the areas where you might usefully challenge clients and have offered some general guidelines for the manner in which you might challenge. There are, however, a number of alternative challenging strategies and it is to these that I now want to turn.

Confrontation

To confront means, among other things, to encounter or to be face to face with. Specifically, I use the term to mean helping clients to identify and face the distortions, ruses and discrepancies which keep them from effective change. Confrontation is a strategy which uses both reflective and probing skills to call attention to perceived incongruities, discrepancies or 'smoke-screens', for the purpose of deeper exploration and understanding. People often become clients because they do not think there is any way out of their problems. Certainly, all problems have an element of inescapability in them, otherwise they would not be problems. Nevertheless, clients are often unaware or only dimly aware of how they disempower themselves. Your task in confronting clients is to help them to understand how their 'faulty' or 'distorted' views are immobilising them.

Consider the following example. A client, Anna, was exploring a work relationship. Her colleague was continually letting her down, by not turning up and double booking. She revealed that she covered for him and took work from him that he had not completed to date. She was angry and resentful. The counsellor thought she was rescuing him.

> *Counsellor*: You sound furious with him and you bail him out regularly, it seems.
> *Anna*: [*angrily*] I can't just do nothing when he doesn't turn up. Other people are being let down and it causes problems. I'm also responsible for seeing that work gets done and I just can't leave it.
> *Counsellor*: You say you 'can't leave it'. What do you imagine would happen if you did that?
> *Anna*: Well, I suppose clients would complain and the department would get a bad name . . . and I haven't thought any further than that.
> *Counsellor*: So, you're protecting everyone, the department and clients, him and yourself.
> *Anna*: Well, yes I am! I like to think of myself as responsible. There's nothing wrong with that, is there? You're suggesting that when he makes a blunder, I should let him sort it out, are you?
> *Counsellor*: I'm not suggesting anything at the moment. It almost sounds as if you think he'd be incapable of sorting his mess out. Does that make any sense?
> *Anna*: [*sheepishly*] I suppose he'd sort his blunders out. He'd have to. I get a real 'high' out of being efficient and, I don't know, being *the* person who can sort things out.
> *Counsellor*: And you can't be efficient and responsible without rescuing him?
> *Anna*: [*laughing*] Sounds like it! Of course I can. And I think I'll stop bailing him out as from now.

Anna's view of the problem was 'distorted' or 'askew'. The counsellor's confrontation helped her to realise that she had a choice about how much she helped her colleague. She could be efficient and responsible without rushing to his rescue and she had been assuming helplessness on his part.

Confronting discrepancies   Clients may, with or without awareness, present you with discrepant messages. Discrepancies may be between

- client's views of themselves and how others see them;
- how clients are and what they wish to be;
- clients' verbal and non-verbal behaviour;
- what clients say they want and what they are doing to get it.

The following are some brief examples:

- Tom sees himself as consultative, his colleagues see him as indecisive.
- Peter says he wants to manage his anxiety about exams yet he makes no attempt to participate in any classes specifically for exam management skills.
- Catherine says she is happy in her relationship, yet she looks downcast and sits with her arms folded and fists clenched.
- Jack says everything at work is fine with a sneer and a hollow laugh.

Let us see how a discrepancy between what a client says he wants and what he is doing to achieve it might be confronted.

The client, Ray, who is in his forties, is discussing his work future.

> *Ray*: [*slowly and forcefully*] I'd really like to give up my job and buy a smallholding somewhere. We'd really like to live in the country and . . . not exactly be self sufficient . . . but live by doing craft work. I keep looking at the price of property and it's still rising. I hope it comes off. We'd both like a place of our own. We've wanted this for some time – it's our dream. It keeps us going.
>
> *Counsellor*: Ray, you said 'I hope it comes off'. It's as if you're telling me that getting what you want is dependent on hope rather than anything you can do. I'm not sure if that's how you see the future.
>
> *Ray*: I haven't done anything yet. I am hoping – to keep me going. If I find out it's impossible, then I won't have anything much to look forward to.

The counsellor focusses on an apparent contradiction. Ray is expressing keenness but doing nothing. Her challenge prompted a realisation that in keeping his plans as 'dreams', he was protecting himself from the possibility of disappointment.

You may also confront the 'excuses' or 'pretexts' that clients use and which prevent them from coping effectively with their concerns. These include:

1 *rationalising*. Clients may excuse or justify their positions by
   diminishing the importance of their concerns. For example,
   Brian, who was out of work, struggling financially and feeling
   low, told his counsellor that he was glad this had happened,
   because he could now talk much more sympathetically to others
   with problems;
2 *delaying*. Some clients will avoid seeing the urgency of a
   situation and put off taking any action. Paula, for example, was
   pregnant and did not know whether to have a termination. She
   guessed several weeks earlier that she was pregnant, but had
   neither consulted her doctor nor discussed it with her counsellor
   till now;
3 *blaming others*. Clients may tell you that others need to act and
   then the problem would be solved. It may well be that, if the
   other people in the situation acted differently, then the problem
   might be overcome. However, clients can use this to avoid acting
   differently themselves. For example, Rosemary was talking
   about her partner. She told the counsellor that he was preventing them from sharing feelings because he was very 'closed'. He
   rarely said what he felt or expressed emotion.

Confronting strengths   Clients often have strengths and resources
which they overlook. Acknowledging their strengths can help
clients to understand themselves differently. The following example
illustrates this.

A client, Brenda, had recently obtained a position as personal
assistant to a company director. She was not coping in her job and
felt very distressed. She revealed that her boss was unhappy with
her work and that he had alerted the personnel department. Her
job had grown since she had taken it, because her boss had taken
on new responsibilities. She described him as 'a lovely man' whom
everyone respected. She had recently moved house on the strength
of her promotion. She feared that a job change might mean less
money and losing her house and garden which she loved. She lived
alone and said that she felt unsupported in her life.

> *Counsellor*: You don't have support at home or at work from what
> you've said. It sounds like your boss expects you to cope.
> *Brenda*: [*angrily*] No, I'm not supported. He never tells me what to do.
> He never says what's priority and what isn't. He complains that I'm
> not quick enough and yet he expects me to listen . . . to sit and talk.
> I get no guidance because he's not there half the time. One of the
> other secretaries said the way to handle him is to cosset him!
> *Counsellor*: You're angry with him and don't sound like you want to
> cosset him. From what you've said so far, you seem to have shown

initiative and ability in getting things for yourself – a new job, a new home, a garden which you are looking forward to organising. I may be wrong but I don't hear you talking about using your initiative with your boss.

Brenda: Yes! You're right. I do have initiative.

Counsellor: And you're waiting for him to tell you what to do.

Brenda: That's not using my initiative, is it?

Brenda then went on to explore what she would like her work life to be like; how she could develop a work plan to submit to her boss rather than ask him to plan with her or for her. She thought that, if her work situation did not improve, she would leave as soon as she found another job, knowing that she had done what she could to effect change.

The counsellor helped Brenda to focus on strength which she was not using. She challenged in a tentative way by using paraphrasing and checking statements before offering her own perspective. Brenda began to see a way out of what previously seemed to her a hopeless situation.

Self-confrontation Finally, you may want to encourage clients to confront themselves in a responsible way, as an alternative to self-blame. Clients may be hard on themselves, but self-blame generally fails to promote greater self-understanding. You might ask them to talk to themselves as a person who is interested in understanding rather than condemning might do. Consider the following example:

Dave: I never learn. It's like I'm on automatic pilot. It's not as if I don't know what to do. But, instead of saying 'No', I grin like a clown and say 'Yes'. So now I'm lumbered again. I'm doing something I don't want to do and I'm angry with myself for being spineless.

Counsellor: You sound hard on yourself. What would you say to yourself, if you described your actions in a kinder and more understanding way?

Dave: I don't know . . . I suppose I'd say, 'You made a mistake. You knew what you wanted to do and you didn't do it. You ignored yourself again and now you're feeling resentful.' As I was saying 'Yes', I thought, 'I don't want to do this, but I ought to help out. It's mean not to.'

Counsellor: Refusing requests is being mean, is it?

The invitation to Dave to talk from a more understanding perspective helps him to shift from self-blame to greater self-understanding. He now has a better idea of how he sabotages his attempts to say what he wants.

I have discussed some of the different ways in which confronting enables you to challenge clients. I now want to look at how providing clients with feedback constitutes another strategy for challenging.

Giving feedback

Giving feedback challenges clients' self-understanding by providing them with information about how another, the counsellor, experiences them. Consider the following example.

A client, Christopher, is facing an important interview for a course. He is concerned that he will not be able to answer his interviewers well enough to obtain a place. He has talked clearly and sensibly about the preparation he has done and the way he will tackle the interview.

> *Christopher*: The problem is that I get muddled and my mind goes blank. I don't seem to be able to get my thoughts in order.

The counsellor decides to challenge by giving Christopher some feedback.

> *Counsellor*: You've given me a very clear outline of what you've done to prepare for the interview. You've also stated how you will handle certain questions, if asked. You're telling me you can't think. It seems to me you're thinking very clearly.

Christopher's view of his behaviour is at odds with the way he is actually behaving. The counsellor's view helps him to begin to see his behaviour in a different light. He also begins to explore how he lives up to his idea of himself as a 'muddler'.

Guidelines for giving feedback   The following are some guidelines for giving feedback (Hopson and Scally, 1982).

1 *Do not label the client.*   For example, being called manipulative or insensitive is both attacking and unhelpful. Clients are likely to want to defend themselves rather than listen to the feedback. Describe the client's behaviour rather than labelling the person. For example, instead of

> *Counsellor*: You're very blaming. No wonder your children don't confide in you.

you might say something like,

> *Counsellor*: I notice you sounded angry when you described your children as secretive. I wonder if they see you as blaming them. What do you think?

2 *Be concrete.*   Describe your client's behaviour clearly and specifically. For example, telling clients that they are avoiding

does not give them much indication of what they are doing and what they might change.

3 *Own your feedback.* This means saying what you think and feel and owning it as such. Begin your feedback with some of the statements outlined in Chapter 3 such as 'I notice', 'I think' or 'I feel'.

4 *Do not blame or condemn.* State clearly what you think and describe the consequences of the client's behaviour. Feedback, as in the following example, can be attacking rather than challenging:

> *Counsellor*: You never express your feelings here. If that is what you do at home, then it's no surprise, is it, that your marriage is so unsatisfactory. Perhaps if you started being more open and less rigid, you would be more at ease with your wife.

Put without blame, it might sound something like this:

> *Counsellor*: I'm aware that you are prepared to talk thoughtfully about what you do, but you don't say how you feel or express your feelings. I find it hard to know what's really important for you and I wonder if your wife does too?

5 *Offer positive as well as negative feedback.* By this, I mean giving balanced feedback that helps clients towards a clearer understanding of their resources and strengths as well as their deficits. I do not mean prefacing any challenging remarks with hollow praise. Clients can also begin to change by doing more of what is positive rather than concentrating solely on obliterating the negative. Finally, you will need to check that clients have heard your feedback by inviting discussion of what you have said.

Providing information

Clients may lack information which would help them to reassess their concerns. Let us consider the following examples.

A bereaved client, Daphne, says that she cannot understand her reactions; her feelings are so intense and sometimes so negative. Giving her some information about what typically happens to those who are bereaved, along with some notion of the tasks which individuals face, may help Daphne to understand herself in the process. She may then feel more able to express what she feels without so much guilt and self-deprecation.

Richard is a trainee on a counselling course. He is finding some of the practical work difficult and wonders if he will ever do well enough to gain his diploma. The following information might well help him:

- what other students typically feel at this stage in the course;
- what problems students confront when they attempt to change aspects of their counselling style;
- a clear assessment from a tutor as to how he is seen by those who will be responsible for his assessment;
- how many students withdraw or fail.

Information may help clients to see themselves and their concerns differently. The student in the preceding example came for a tutorial thinking he was a failure. Exploring the information he was given helped him to see himself as someone who was confronting the typical problems which accompany a skills training. The information also helped him to focus on which aspects of his counselling performance he could usefully improve.

Guidelines for providing information   The following are some guidelines for providing information.

1 *Make sure the information is relevant.* For example, the student Richard does not need information on drop-out rates from undergraduate courses.
2 *Do not overload the client with detail.* There is a limit to what people can remember and assimilate.
3 *Make sure the client understands what you are saying.* Therefore, present the information clearly, avoid jargon and invite questions. You might want to ask clients to summarise what you have said.
4 *Help the client to use the information.* Information of itself does not solve problems. For example, simply telling clients about a transition model or the tasks facing them at this particular developmental stage in their lives will not make them more skilled, or more competent to deal with their concerns. You may need to help clients to see the relevance of the information and to explore what new light it throws on their concerns.
5 *Do not confuse information with advice.* Recommending or advising may have a place in counselling with some clients. I do not think there is anything wrong with giving clear, relevant advice to a client which is based on your knowledge of that client and your expertise. Giving information is not the same as telling clients what you think they might do.

Giving directives
Directives are the most influencing of all the challenging strategies. As the label suggests, the counsellor openly directs the client to do something. Ivey et al. (1987) provide many examples of directives

which counsellors of different theoretical orientations typically use. This skill is typically used in the Middle Stage of counselling when the counsellor has made some assessment as to what it would be most appropriate to direct the client to do. Directives are intended to help clients discover new insights and awareness in what they bring to counselling. The following example demonstrates how giving directives challenges clients.

A client, Peter, is talking about being excluded by his partner. He recounts, in a level and balanced way, what to the counsellor seem hurtful experiences.

> *Counsellor*: [*gently*] Put some feelings to those words. [*gives a directive*]
> *Peter*: I don't know, hurt and sad, I suppose.
> *Counsellor*: Stay with those feelings for a moment; experience what you feel. [*gives another directive*]
> *Peter*: [*sits quietly for a moment*] Actually, I feel angry. As I think about what he did and how insensitive he's been, [*much louder*] I feel really furious. How could he be so inconsiderate?

Here the counsellor uses directives to help Peter identify and express what he feels. He shifts from not displaying much emotion to labelling and giving vent to his emotions.

Clients often give clues as to how they avoid taking responsibility for themselves and deny their ability to change in the language they use. For example they may say 'I can't', 'I have to' or 'I should'. In each instance, you may direct them by inviting them to experience saying 'I won't', 'I choose to' or 'I want to' respectively.

Guidelines for giving directives   The following are some guidelines for giving directives.

1 *Do not overuse.* Clients may feel persecuted, if they are constantly on the receiving end of directives. Too liberal a use of directives can rob clients of control and may encourage dependence.

2 *Be clear about your intentions.* Before you direct clients, ask yourself whether doing this will help them to see their concerns from a different and more liberating angle.

3 *Check with clients first.* You can ask clients if they would be willing, for example, to do an exercise or a role-play.

4 *Be prepared for clients to say 'No!'* Clients may resist doing what you ask. If this occurs, you may want to explore what they experienced in the interchange. You may need to accept that you have been heavy-handed or intrusive. Trust may be an issue for some clients. They may not trust that you will be able to offer them the protection which they think they will need; or

they may not trust that the technique you are suggesting will be useful to them.

5   *Keep your voice calm and direct*. Saying 'Put some words to that feeling' in a stentorian tone may well either antagonise or frighten clients.

6   *Give clear guidelines*. A counsellor reported that she asked a client to take himself back to when he was 9 years old. She said 'Take your time and think your way into your childhood, *a bit*.' The client did just that. He thought a bit, then said the exercise was difficult and did not want to do it. Clearer instructions would have been something like: 'I want you to imagine that you are 9 years old. Now take your time. Sit as you imagine you sat when you were little. When you are ready, look at yourself and describe what you are wearing.' Here the counsellor gives the client space and some clear guidelines which help him to begin to relive a time when he was small.

Counsellor self-disclosure

This strategy occurs when, in order to challenge and to promote new awareness, you share with your clients some experiences in your own life. Because the effect is to shift the focus from client to counsellor, it should be used sparingly. The counselling relationship is one of limited reciprocity and dwelling for too long on your own trials and successes is unhelpful and often unwelcome. In one sense, of course, you cannot avoid disclosing yourself to clients, both by your self-presentation and what you say and do. Before offering some guidelines for self-disclosure, I want to look briefly at two examples and identify in what way self-disclosure both challenges and promotes new awareness.

Example 1   Beverley is discussing her work. She has taken a job which she dislikes intensely and from which she is attempting to escape.

> *Beverley*: It's as if I've gone against what I *ought* to do by taking this job. I feel as if I've rebelled and now I'm paying for it.
> *Counsellor*: You haven't done what your parents expected, is that it?
> *Beverley*: I can't remember them ever saying I should do this or that. They used to say, 'The important thing is that you're happy.'
> *Counsellor*: My parents used to say to me 'Do whatever you like. It's alright by us', and I knew that what they really meant was 'as long as it involves being in the medical profession'. Does that make any sense to you?
> *Beverley*: That's it exactly. When you said that, I realised that this job wasn't a step up the ladder, more money or more responsibility . . . in other words, none of things they would approve of. They've never

said that in so many words but that is what they wanted for me. I don't think I'm very good at rebelling either. This is the first time I've tried it on the job front and look what happens. I fall flat on my face!

The counsellor's self-disclosure was short and relevant. She responded to Beverley's comment about what she 'ought' to have done. Instead of questioning, she thought that an example from her own life might help Beverley to begin to understand her behaviour in a different way.

Example 2   Simon is putting a brave face on his misery. He is being stalwart in describing a particularly painful episode. In response to the counsellor's statement, 'I imagine you felt sad', Simon continues with:

> *Simon*: [*regretfully*] These things happen, don't they? That's life . . . and you just have to get on with it. Dwelling on the past won't change anything. Neither will moaning about it.

The counsellor notices that Simon has avoided talking about or expressing his feelings. Furthermore, he has distanced himself from the issue by saying 'you' when he is actually referring to himself and what he believes. Instead of using a directive, such as 'Will you say "I'm going to get on with life"?' or a paraphrase, such as 'You want to get on with life and not be hampered by feelings', she decides that self-disclosure may help him to express what he is hinting at:

> *Counsellor*: I think that, if I'd experienced the rejection that you've experienced, I would feel sad and hurt. I've also wanted to push away painful feelings. I wonder if that is how it is for you?
> *Simon*: I suppose I don't want to seem weak and – don't laugh – but I feel that if I got really sad I would never be able to stop and I'd never be happy again. I do feel wretched and also angry.

Here the counsellor used self-disclosure to model talking about feelings. Sometimes clients lack the skill of making feeling statements. They have had little practice at identifying, labelling and expressing their feelings. They lack what Steiner (1984) calls 'emotional literacy'. The counsellor's self-disclosure enabled Simon to begin to feel safe enough to identify and explore his feelings.

How to self-disclose

1 *Be brief*. Talking at length about yourself may burden clients and make you seem inexpert. Also, describing how you solved your problems can be daunting for some clients who may need to set small goals and take change in small steps.
2 *Tailor your self-disclosure*. By this I mean use language and

experiences with which clients can identify. Telling a client who is on Income Support that you understand what it is like to be short of money . . . 'because £15,000 per year really doesn't go anywhere irrespective of what some people think' . . . does not show much understanding of the client's world and is unhelpful.

3   *Understand your client first.* You will be in a position to offer self-disclosure effectively, if you have a clear understanding of how clients see their concerns and have listened carefully to what they may be implying or overlooking.

4   *Be direct.* Use 'I' and describe the experience clearly. End your statement by returning the focus to your client.

5   *Be clear about your motives.* Are your disclosing to help the client or to unburden yourself? If the disclosure is to relieve your own feelings, then it is more appropriately discussed either in supervision or in counselling for yourself (Hawkins and Shohet, 1989).

Finally, let us turn now to a strategy which invites reassessment by focussing on what is happening in the relationship between you and your clients. It is one which is surprisingly powerful.

Immediacy
Immediacy means focussing on what your clients are thinking and feeling 'now' and on what is happening in the counselling relationship between you. Clients will talk about past and current events in their lives. They will also speculate about the future, and certainly, setting goals with them is future orientated. The place for discussion of the past and planning for the future is 'the now' and, in fact, these issues cannot be discussed anywhere else. However, clients may not be aware of how they are feeling 'right now' and they may gain a new awareness by staying with and exploring their thoughts, feelings and behaviour as they occur 'now'. Let us look at an example of immediacy which attempts to assist a client to focus on what is going on for her now.

The client, Diana, was talking about how she would cope with a forthcoming important event at work. She was describing, in a bombastic way, how she would handle the meeting. The counsellor thought that the brusque words might be a mask for fear. Certainly, the client had talked about 'getting in first'.

Diana: [*with a sigh*] I'll just say what I think and, if they don't like it, well that's too bad!
Counsellor: You seemed deflated as you said that and I wonder what you're feeling now?
Diana: Like the wind's been taken out of my sails.

Counsellor: Without power? [*Diana nods.*] What are you feeling at this moment?

Diana: Scared, frightened. I can see their faces and the grey suits and hear the questions. When I reply, it's as if I know nothing and I'm talking incoherently . . . [*begins to cry*] . . . Whatever I say will be dismissed as wrong.

Counsellor: Sounds like you see yourself on trial and you're frightened. [*Client nods*] What are you saying to yourself?

Diana: [*thoughtfully and slowly*] I'm a failure . . . useless and I don't deserve to succeed. They all know more than me and I'll show my ignorance. I won't be able to control my fear.

The counsellor and Diana went on to explore her thoughts. The counsellor asked her to compare the frightening fantasy with what had actually happened so far in her work life. She was able to gain a more objective view of herself as someone who was knowledgeable and had achieved. She realised that, though collectively a committee may have greater breadth of knowledge than her, that did not make her stupid or a failure.

Immediacy can also be used to focus on the relationship between counsellor and client. Exploring what happens in this relationship may help clients to gain a clearer understanding of what happens in their other relationships. You may explore what is happening at the moment between you and clients or what you discern as patterns that you see emerging in the relationship. Let us look at an example of immediacy in which the focus is the pattern which seems to be emerging in the counselling relationship.

A client, Harry, is talking about supporting others, especially his mother and his girl-friend. He says that one of his strengths is being able to listen to others and gain their confidence. The counsellor thinks that he supports others at a cost to himself. He is looking tired and has not wanted to focus on himself. He is prepared to talk about what he does.

Counsellor: I'm thinking, 'I wonder who supports you?'

Harry: [*sharply*] I've got friends, you know that. Anyway, [*with a hostile smile*] isn't this what counselling's all about, you listening to me?

Counsellor: I think you're telling me that talking about support for yourself is a 'no-go area'.

Harry: It's not that. Other people have got enough on their plates without listening to me all day. It's not as if I'm very depressed or redundant or homeless, is it? You know, in dire straits?

Counsellor: I don't think receiving support is conditional on severe problems. I'd like to say what I think happens between us. I've noticed that you find it hard to receive support from me to the extent that you cover your feelings of hurt with either anger or a joke. I notice that if I really try to understand you, you push me away with a laugh or throw-away line. Perhaps, I've moved in too close too quickly and not respected your pace enough. Does what I've said make any sense to you?

Harry: Sometimes you really understand me and I feel caught out! I feel anxious telling you this, because I know it isn't true . . . but it's like you can see right through me and see that I'm weak. So, I guess I avoid sharing what I think and feel. Sometimes you push me and I don't like that.

The counsellor uses immediacy to focus on a pattern. Harry continues by exploring how admitting he wants support is a sign of weakness for him. It also involves sharing what he thinks and feels. Moving closer to others raises the possibility of rejection.

When to use immediacy

1 *When trust is an issue*. Clients may not be involving themselves in the counselling process, because they do not see the counsellor as trustworthy or they are anxious about forming a close, trusting relationship. For example, Wendy believes that, if she shows how distressed she is, the counsellor will not be able to cope.

Counsellor: Wendy, I sense you don't feel safe enough with me to tell me how unhappy you are. I wonder what you imagine would happen between us, if you shared your sadness.

2 *When the client and counsellor are stuck*. Consider the following example. A client, Rachel, was talking about her lover and whether or not they would live together. The counsellor became aware that she was feeling detached and the conversation was about what Rachel's partner might or might not decide.

Counsellor: Rachel, I'm aware that, as we've been talking, I've felt uninvolved and I've realised that we're talking about what Neil may or may not decide. It's as if we are both sitting here waiting for him to make a move. What's your view?

3 *When there are boundary issues*. Clients may want the counselling relationship to spill over into a friendship or a sexual relationship. If you sense that this is the case, then you will need to check with your client your understanding of what is happening and either clarify or restate the boundaries of the relationship. For example:

Keith: I think we get on really well together. It's a shame we only meet once a week. I've realised you don't often see me when I'm happy either.

Counsellor: I think it's important that we maintain our relationship as a counselling relationship. I'm not sure if you're saying you'd like our relationship to develop differently. Perhaps that's an issue for us to explore. What do you think?

Finally, immediacy is a powerful strategy because it faces both you and client with the dynamics of your relationship. It is difficult for clients to remain distant when they are faced with a non-defensive request to explore the counselling relationship.

Guidelines for immediacy
– be assertive. Say directly what you think, feel and observe;
– be open yourself. Immediacy is not telling clients what they are doing that is counter-productive. If a pattern is developing between you and clients, then you have some part in that development;
– describe what you think is happening clearly and specifically. Say what you think the client is doing and what you are doing;
– ask the client to comment on what you have said.

What happens if you do not challenge clients?
Reassessment by challenging is a process which takes time and usually involves gradual '*cognitive shifts*' for clients. Failure to challenge may mean that counselling becomes circular and clients do not gain the new insights required for goal setting and change. In one sense, the entire counselling process is challenging, because from the outset clients are brought face to face with their concerns. However, unless you influence clients to adopt different perspectives, they are unlikely to move beyond their present limiting views; those views which are keeping them trapped or immobilised. Challenging requires clients to look anew at themselves and their concerns as a necessary precursor to change.

Summary

This chapter has been about challenging clients, the purpose of which is to invite deeper exploration. This means enabling them to 'go below the surface'; to explore and articulate those aspects of themselves and their concerns of which they are either unaware or dimly aware. The outcome of using the challenging strategies is that they will have a new, different and more empowering perspective on their concerns. In effect, they will have reassessed their position.

Reassessment is not an end in itself. It is useful in so far as it enables clients to see possibilities for change. Some clients may leave counselling, having adopted a different perspective on themselves and their concerns. Others may need help to decide what they want to change and to plan how to effect that change. The next chapter discusses how to work with clients to plan change and take action.

5 The Ending Stage: Action and Closure

The Ending Stage

Aims
- to decide on appropriate change
- to implement change
- to transfer learning
- to end the counselling relationship

Strategies
- goal setting
- action planning
- evaluating action and sustaining change
- closure

Skills
Using the basic sequences for listening and challenging

In this chapter, I begin by discussing the aims of the Ending Stage and proceed to review the strategies by which these aims will be attained. I will concentrate more on strategies than on skills, because once you have mastered the basic skill sequences which enable you to facilitate exploration and reassessment, you will be well equipped to assist clients in the process of setting goals, planning and taking appropriate action (Munro et al., 1989).

The Ending Stage of counselling typically deals with goals, action and closure. As a result of the work done in the two preceding stages, clients will have gained the kind of clearer understanding of themselves and their concerns which provide the impetus for change. Planning and taking effective action are made more possible because of the work done in the Beginning and Middle Stages. Some clients, of course, may choose not to travel any further with you. Once they have explored their problems and gained a new view, they see clearly what they want to do and set about achieving it. Others will need help to decide what change they want and support while they try out new behaviours.

Aims

I have identified the following four aims to guide the counselling work of the Ending Stage. These are:

1 to decide on appropriate change;
2 to implement change;
3 to transfer learning;
4 to end the counselling relationship.

Let us look at these in turn.

To decide on appropriate change

If clients are to cope more effectively with their concerns or solve their problems, they will need to do two things: first, they will need to identify the specific changes they want to make, and second, they will need to check that those changes will have the particular impact that they want on their problems. The fact that clients have explored and reassessed their concerns usually means that they are inclined towards change and can see the potential action. However, that does not necessarily mean that they will know precisely *what* change they want to make. Nor does it mean that they know *how* to implement that change. To assume otherwise risks overlooking an important step in the counselling process. Changing generally involves risks and losses as well as benefits and gains. In addition to identifying what positive outcomes they seek, you will need to help your clients to decide what risks and costs are manageable for them. Helping clients to decide on appropriate change means helping them to assess whatever outcomes they want, which are within their resources and with costs and benefits that are acceptable.

To implement change

This may sound obvious but clients must act if they want to change. They must stop doing some things and start doing others. For example, a client who wishes to lose weight will need to change her habits in some way. Your task will be to help clients both to decide on what action to take and to take that action. This involves exploring different options, choosing ones which seem appropriate as well as timing and sequencing any action. Occasionally, you may want to rehearse with clients or engage in some role-play as a preparation. Also, clients may fail to implement changes because they do not have a reward or support system to sustain them. An important aspect of facilitating change is to attend to the rewards and pay-offs which will accrue to clients.

To transfer learning

Through the processes of exploration and challenging, clients learn about aspects of themselves and their behaviour. They may identify resources which they have not been using fully as well as skills which they may need to develop. A basic assumption of counselling is that clients will be able to transfer their learning from counselling to situations outside of it. Consider the following examples.

Rod learned to express his feelings appropriately in counselling. His counsellor helped Rod to explore not only how he denied his feelings but typically when and with whom. In order to enable him to transfer his learning about himself and the new skills he had acquired, they explored how he might confront situations both at work and at home in a more appropriate way.

Gina discovered that her resentment with her partner had much to do with her tendency to rescue him. She used counselling to explore other ways of relating to her partner which did not involve treating him as a helpless victim, even when he solicited it. Gina also realised that her tendency to take over and to act as though others could not manage on their own was a pattern in her life. She was able to transfer her learning in counselling not only to her interactions with her partner but also to other relationships.

Helping clients to transfer their learning may involve identifying obstacles to change and planning how to overcome or minimise those obstacles. It can, also, involve coaching clients in new behaviour.

Finally, your clients will take away a 'mental picture' of you. An internalised view of the counsellor will give some clients a resource which they can access when confronting future problems and decisions. A colleague revealed that he frequently asked himself what his counsellor might say to him. In doing this, he gave himself the space to think through what he wanted and so avoided doing what he thought he 'should' do. Teaching clients this counselling model can also provide them with knowledge that they can use to tackle other issues which face them now or in the future.

To end the counselling relationship

The Ending Stage of counselling, in addition to goal setting and action planning, has to do with ending the relationship. For most counsellors and clients ending means recognising the loss of the relationship as well as celebrating clients' new learning. I think endings deserve as much thought and attention as beginnings. For some clients, it may be a painful time which contains echoes of other difficult endings that they have experienced in their lives. It is important, therefore, that they are given the opportunity to explore what the end of the counselling relationship means for them and to plan a 'good' ending with you.

Endings may also prove a sad time for counsellors. You will have grown close to clients and even though their work with you has been completed, you will inevitably miss some of them. While it is inappropriate to burden them with your feelings, it is important nonetheless to recognise that endings mean loss for you. If indeed this is the case, you will provide good modelling for your clients by disclosing in a direct and appropriate way that you will miss them and have valued the efforts they have made to change and grow.

Of course, not all endings are a time of satisfying reflection. There may be times when clients want to end prematurely. They may not have achieved what they wanted because in spite of your best efforts, they have been reluctant to tackle their concerns. Clients may sometimes think that you are not helping them and decide they want to work with another counsellor. You may also have occasion to refer them to someone else, because you feel that the issues which they bring are beyond your current experience and expertise. However, you will have been an important person in your departing clients' lives. The end of this special relationship needs to be recognised just as much as the end of the counselling work.

Let us turn now to the strategies which are instrumental in achieving the counselling aims of the ending stage.

Strategies

Goal setting

The work of the preceding two stages involves helping clients to understand themselves in such a way that they can see change as a possibility. Goal setting provides a rational strategy for helping clients both to generate and to decide on options for change.

Consider the following example. The client, Daniel, sought counselling because he was lonely. He had few friends and often felt intensely sad. He wanted his life to be different, he wanted a partner, friends and to feel valued by others. At the start of counselling, the perspective he offered on his concerns may be summarised as follows:

> I want to be happier. I can't remember ever being wanted. My parents separated when I was 3 years old and I suppose I've never learned to trust anyone. If I'd had a stable secure childhood, then I wouldn't have

the problems that I have now; and I wouldn't be so lonely and depressed.

In the Beginning Stage, Daniel talked about his past. His view or frame of reference was that he was the product of his early childhood experiences; and those experiences were responsible for his current status. He wanted life to be different but did not know how to effect change. The counsellor hypothesised that Daniel had a view of himself as unlovable and of the world as a hostile place. She noticed that he found it hard to trust her and that he withdrew whenever she attempted to get close to him.

As the counselling progressed, the counsellor challenged Daniel. She focussed on their relationship and explored with him how he seemed to want to be close to her and for her to understand him, but when she did he pulled away. He understood that this was the strategy he adopted with others. He realised that intimate friendships were frightening, because he risked being rejected and hurt. Daniel became aware of how, as a bewildered child, this had been important for his self-preservation, but that now he was not in such a powerless position. The counsellor also encouraged him to explore how his self-estimation inhibited him in being open and taking risks with others. In her interactions with him, she pointed out how he avoided hearing praise from her. They agreed that she would point out each time he ignored positive feedback from her or dismissed his achievements.

From the work of the Middle Stage, Daniel gained a different and more liberating view of himself. He modified his beliefs about himself and others. He saw how he had allowed his past to keep him stuck in loneliness. However, now he had this altered perspective, the question remained of what he wanted to accomplish and how he would accomplish it. Daniel and his counsellor turned translating his aim of 'a happier life, with close friends and a stable partnership' into goals.

Goals are *what* the client wants to achieve. Action plans are the '*how*', that is they state specifically *how* clients will reach their goals. In general, identifying clear outcomes helps clients to avoid ineffective action. However, sometimes acting first and reflecting on the outcomes helps clients to gain a clearer idea of what they want to achieve. For example, a client who is unhappy in his current employment may gain a clearer understanding of the satisfactions he seeks by applying for other positions and going for interviews. Testing the market may also help him to decide what change is possible. Let us turn now to the goal-setting framework.

Developing goals   If goals are to be both practicable and feasible, they will need to fulfil several criteria (Brammer, 1988):

1   goals should be wanted by the client;
2   goals must be tailored by the client;
3   goals need to be observable and assessable.

Let us look at these in turn.

1   *Goals should be wanted by the client.* This means helping clients to discover what they want to achieve and which, out of all the possible outcomes, they value most. Making changes takes time and energy and clients are likely to work harder for goals that are their own. They are less likely to sustain their investment in pursuing ends which they do not value or which they see as imposed upon them. You will need to be alert to any hints or clues which clients give that communicate their lack of involvement in the options they mention. The following are examples of the statements that clients might make which suggest that they are not following their own wishes, and of possible counsellor responses:

Geoff: My partner and I have talked about the future and she thinks I should take early retirement.
Counsellor: Early retirement is what your partner prefers. I'm not sure if that's what you want too?;

and where the clues might primarily be non-verbal:

Andrea: [*looking fed up and sounding bored*] I suppose the way out of this predicament is to save more money.
Counsellor: You sound as though that idea doesn't have much appeal. I wonder if there are other options.

Sometimes, however, clients say quite openly that what they are planning to achieve is not what they want but either what others want or what they think they 'ought' to do. Your influence will be confined to inviting clients to explore their 'shoulds' and the costs and benefits of the outcomes they have raised.

Another aspect of goal setting may be helping clients to clarify their values. Goals are more likely to be achieved if they are in keeping with clients' *values*. For example, a client, Victor, tells his counsellor that he has looked forward to his retirement. However, he now faces redundancy, which means retiring two years earlier than he had anticipated. The news has been a great shock to him. Now that he is actually confronted with a future without work, he begins to examine just what work means to him and what he will do without it.

Clients are more likely to review their values in times of change or transition than at other times in their lives (Sugarman, 1986). Planning change may throw into sharper relief values which clients had previously considered less significant.

Helping clients to identify outcomes which they want does not mean that they ignore the wishes of important people in their lives. Rather it means that, if they are helped to separate out what they want from the expectations of others, they will be in a position to make an informed choice. This in turn is likely to have the effect of freeing them from believing that they have no other options but to do what others expect of them. Challenging clients to test out their assumptions is one way of helping them to distinguish between their own and others' expectations.

Another way is to do a simple balance sheet. For example, Anita's goal was to increase her part-time employment to full time. Her counsellor asked her to estimate the positive and negative effects of this option as follows:

Positive	*Negative*
Develop skills	Won't be in when son (aged
Feel more confident in myself	12) gets home from school
Finances improved	Miss seeing friends in the day
Feel more independent	Don't think I'll get much help
Feel useful	with domestic chores
	Partner not too keen

Anita realised that, while this was an important goal for her, she did not know how her partner and son would view certain implications of her decision. Working full time would mean she had less time for work in the home. Rearranging the domestic tasks had not been discussed in the family. It will be hard for clients to achieve their objectives, if other people who are close to them either fail to support them or sabotage their efforts.

2   *Goals must be tailored by the client.* Tailoring goals means shaping them so that they become specific and realistic. Let us consider what each of these terms means.

(a)   '*specific*': Vague goals are unlikely to lead to effective action and change. For example, a client may make a statement like: 'I can understand now how I've let work take over my life and I do want a better social life and a better balance in my life.' This is a useful starting point for tailoring goals. However, it is vague and needs refining. For example, what does a 'better balance' and a 'better social life' actually mean for this client? Unless she specifies this, how will she know what action to take and, equally importantly, how will she know when she has achieved what she wants?

The client, Linda, is in a relationship which she finds unsatisfying. She feels neglected and dismissed by Paul, her partner. Through a process of exploration and challenging, she comes to realise that she rarely says what she wants to him. She waits for him to take the lead in their decision making and, when she doesn't get what she wants, tells herself she has been too demanding. She begins by saying

Linda: I do want to do something about my relationship. For a start, I want to know if we've got a future together. [*Client makes a vague statement.*]

Counsellor: From what you've said over the previous weeks, it sounds as if leaving the relationship is way down your list of options. If you imagine yourself getting on better with Paul, what would be happening? [*Counsellor uses a hypothetical question to encourage the client to begin to identify some options.*]

Linda: We'd have a closer relationship. I'd be saying what I think and feel. I would take the initiative in making decisions and not wait for him to say what he wants. I realise that I've usually kept quiet about what I want and allowed him to take control of our lives. I want to say what I really think and feel. I want more influence. I want to be equal; not someone who 'tags' along. [*Client becomes more specific.*]

Linda has been encouraged to be more specific about what she wants to accomplish. She has tailored a more specific goal from a vague statement. The goal – to say what she wants, thinks and feels – is within her control. Linda can learn to be more direct and open. She can develop her self-awareness and self-regard if she chooses. In doing this, she may influence Paul's attitude towards her. She realises that she has had little practice at saying what she wants and that in order to begin to take a more active stance with Paul, she will need to develop these skills.

Linda and her counsellor moved on to consider various options for learning and practising a more open and assertive style with Paul.

(b) *'realistic'*: A 'realistic goal' means a goal within the client's resources. It seems obvious to state that clients are unlikely to achieve their goals, if they do not have the emotional, physical, financial and social resources. For example, Ben, who has achieved poor results in his fifth-year examinations, may not have the resources (academic achievement and potential) to enter the sixth form and, subsequently, university.

An important aspect of counselling work in the Beginning and Middle Stages may be to help clients to discover what resources they do have. However, it is important that you keep this in mind when considering goals and action. Clients may overlook or underestimate the importance of the social systems in which they live and work and their previous experiences and achievements.

Clients' attempts to set goals for others also comes within the category of what is unrealistic. Usually, clients have little direct control over the behaviour of others; they have the most control over their own. They may well want to set goals which include changes which they want others to make. This is not to deny that some clients suffer abuse at the hands of other people. However, realistic goals should focus on the clients' behaviour.

Consider the following example. Freda was discussing a work colleague. She told the counsellor how angry she was. Her goal was to give this colleague some feedback and Freda added 'I want him to consider me in future.' The counsellor pointed out that Freda could express her anger and give her feedback, but doing this did not ensure that she would get what she wanted. The focus was shifted to Freda's behaviour and what *she* could do to influence her colleague.

This is not to deny that the behaviour of important others in clients' lives may need to change; but the clients are the ones working with you, not their friends, colleagues or lovers. Clients may of course influence those closest to them to act differently by a change in their own behaviour; but that is less within their control.

You will also be concerned with the adequacy of the goals which clients set. An adequate goal is one that either resolves the problem or helps clients to handle their concerns more effectively. A client, Arthur, for example, tells his counsellor that he wants more free time to develop his social circle. He decides to make available one day per month for leisure activities. This goal, if achieved, may not contribute to resolving his problems of overwork and isolation.

You may want to ask clients the following questions: 'If you achieve this goal, how will that help you to achieve the . . . [*partnership, social life, financial security, increased self-esteem, and so on*] . . . that you say you want?'; or 'Will achieving this outcome help you to cope more effectively with your concerns?'

As a form of self-sabotage, clients may sometimes want to set goals which are unlikely to give them the outcome they say they want. For example, the client, Arthur, who is only prepared to devote one day per month to interests and leisure activities, may not achieve much in that time. He may tell himself that any attempt to get a better social life and make more friends is hopeless. He will then simply return to immersing himself in work.

Finally, working with clients to identify realistic goals means looking at the costs and benefits of achieving this goal as opposed to others. Setting realistic goals means assessing whether or not the cost of achieving a particular outcome would be excessive. For example, Linda – the client who wanted to be more open with her partner – may need to confront the probability that the way things are 'suits' her partner. Any changes that she makes may provoke a split in the relationship. Also, *she* may learn to communicate more effectively but *he* may resolutely seek to maintain the status quo. Challenging clients to grow is an important part of counselling. However, you will need to accept that some clients may not want to achieve what you think is appropriate change. They may be satisfied with a relatively small alteration in their circumstances, because the price of doing otherwise seems exorbitant to them.

This brings us to the final criterion.

3   *Goals need to be observable and assessable.* Goals stated in clear behavioural terms allow both you and your clients to identify yardsticks for assessing what headway they are making. Establishing criteria for assessment allows them to assess both where they are in the process and to know when their goals have been achieved. In other words, when clients have achieved their goals, in what ways will they be behaving differently from the ways in which they are behaving now?

Consider the following example. Gareth wants an easier relationship with his son. His goals are to

– decrease the sarcasm and ridicule he uses;
– distinguish between his son as a person and his son's behaviour;
– give advice when his son asks for it and not before;
– give his opinion as such and not as fact.

Gareth can monitor his behaviour with his son. He will know when he is using less sarcasm and ridicule and being more accepting of his son's views. Others too will be able to see him behaving differently, if he achieves these goals.

Finally, if clients are to bring about change, you will need to challenge them to plan within a realistic time frame. Clients who make statements like 'I'll start eating less when the warmer weather comes' are being vague about the time frame and may never accomplish their goals.

The criteria I have outlined in this section will provide you with an excellent framework for listening to clients and assisting them to create coherent and attainable goals for an improved future.

Exploration and challenging in goal setting   Effective goal setting requires continuing exploration and challenging. It is important that clients are encouraged to express and to explore both feelings and thoughts which may arise at this time. They may have doubts about their ability to implement and sustain action plans, particularly if they have attempted change before and failed. Helping them to explore their fears, their vulnerability at attempting new things and their anxieties about choosing is often part of the process. Neither does goal setting mean that counselling becomes an emotionally barren activity, in which ratings and lists are made, pros and cons weighed up without attention to what clients may be feeling. Indeed, there is some evidence that counsellors high in empathy, warmth and genuineness are more effective in encouraging clients to become involved in goal setting than counsellors rated as lower over these dimensions (Mickelson and Stevic, 1971).

How to set goals   The Beginning and Middle Stages of counselling will help clients to see their concerns from a different perspective and one which is potentially more change orientated. However, they may still not know what they are going to do with this new knowledge. They may say things like: 'I do feel better about myself. I can see that I've put myself down in the past and that is how I've stopped myself from getting what I want'; or 'I'd like to have a better relationship with my son, I can see that I've been a bit hard on him.'

Having outlined, in the previous section, the criteria for feasible goals, I will now consider some of the steps and techniques for helping clients to identify specifically what they want to achieve.

Helping clients to identify options.   Clients are more likely to find ways of solving or coping better with their concerns if they choose from a range of options. There are a number of useful techniques which can help clients to begin to develop goals (Egan, 1985). They include:

- imagining different futures;
- brainstorming;
- sentence completion.

Let us look at each of these in turn

1   *Imagining different futures*. Egan (1986) has called this 'creating new scenarios'. Using this technique involves asking clients to imagine what the future would be like, if they were controlling their problems more effectively or had resolved them. Once clients have identified a range of possible pictures of the future, then they are encouraged to review them and choose one to tailor into workable goals. For example, you may sometimes want to encourage clients to generate several imaginary pictures.

Consider the following. Simon is a teacher who is dissatisfied with the way he is organising his work. During previous sessions, he began to see that he was responsible for the lack of boundaries he placed on his work. He wanted a balance between work and home which meant that his family/social life had more prominence. His 'pictures' are as follows:

- 'I'd be in another job. I'd be working as a computer programmer in a small software writing firm.'
- 'I'd be confining all my preparation and marking to lunch hours and from 5.00 to 6.00 p.m. each evening. I'd work alternate Sundays only.'
- 'I'd have a different timetable within the school, with less responsibility for pastoral work.'
- 'I would be doing the same amount of work in the school, but I'd be worrying less about it. I'd believe that the preparation I'd done would be good enough.'

Simon decides that the second option appeals most to him. He does not want to leave teaching or give up his pastoral role. The option is appraised for realism and effectiveness in coping with the issue which Simon presented.

2   *Brainstorming*. This technique involves asking clients to suspend critical judgement and identify as many possibilities for change as they can. For example, a client, Caroline, who wishes to control her anxiety produced the following list of options:

- be more relaxed;
- become more assertive;
- have an increased social circle and support network;

- stop inhibiting thoughts when they occur;
- have a plan which manages my time more efficiently;
- develop interests which involve other people;
- bring about a gradual decrease in solitary pursuits;
- receive praise for what I do well;
- accept negative feedback and not be depressed by it.

No doubt you will be able to increase the list. Once Caroline has decided *what* she will accomplish to manage her anxiety, she can then decide *how* she will achieve the goal. She may decide that being more relaxed and stopping negative thoughts will help substantially. There are many ways of learning to relax and Caroline will need to decide which action will best suit her. For example, she could buy a commercially made relaxation tape, join a weekend workshop or an evening class in stress management. Some of her action plans may address more than one goal. Joining an evening class may increase her social circle and provide her with the opportunity to obtain praise. This client may decide that all of these goals will help her and, with her counsellor, she can discuss which ones to go for initially. Brainstorming can be a pleasurable activity for clients, because it gives them permission to talk without the usual restraints of evaluating and questioning.

Here is a list of guidelines for brainstorming:

(a) encourage clients to think of as many options as they can and to suspend critical judgment if they begin to evaluate options;

(b) record all options. Do not censor the list either overtly, by failing to record suggestions which you think are useless or unreasonable; or more subtly, by the use of non-verbal cues such as grimacing or sighing heavily;

(c) prompt them by asking 'Who do you know who manages a similar problem to yours? What do they do?'; 'What possibilities are there locally which you could tap into?', and by offering your ideas. You might say something like 'I notice that you haven't mentioned doing . . .';

(d) after each prompt, allow them time to generate further ideas;

(e) ask them what action steps they have rejected in the past;

(f) encourage them to use their imagination in a direct way; for example, you might say, 'Imagine that you are resolving your problem and this time you are doing something completely different; what are you doing?';

(g) reward and support clients by giving positive feedback for their creativity and the energy they are putting into the exercise;

(h) make it pleasurable. I do not mean trivialise but encourage them to feel what power they have in being able to use their thinking skills and their imagination;

(i) do not go on for too long. Clients should not be overwhelmed by the length of the list of possible options for action or harassed to come up with yet another possibility.

The final step is to appraise the list and discard options which are too costly in terms of time and energy or which require resources which the client may not have. For example, a client who wishes to change her job may not have the resources to do that immediately. She may need to retrain or update her existing skills before making applications.

3 *Sentence completion.* This is a simple way of encouraging clients to become more change orientated. It may be used in conjunction with the two preceding techniques. You ask clients to finish sentences.

Consider the following example. A client, Felicity, has decided that she would like to be more sociable and less isolated. She has explored how she stops herself from entering relationships with others and feels confident enough in herself to take the risk of seeking close friendships.

Counsellor: Take your time and finish off the sentences I'll give you. I'll write down what you say and then we'll discuss it.
Felicity: OK.
Counsellor: This is the first sentence, 'If my social life were completely different to the way it is now, I would be . . .'.
Felicity: Well! [*smiles*] I'd be having a wonderful time. Yes. I'd be doing all sorts of exciting things with people I liked.
Counsellor: What sort of things would you be doing?
Felicity: Oh! going to the theatre, sailing, learning to play the piano, brushing up my French. In fact, hearing myself say all of this, I don't know why I don't do these things now. They're not so out of the ordinary; are they?

Felicity and her counsellor review her statements and form a list of possible goals. For example, she decides that she will increase her theatre going. However, the counsellor's hunch is that Felicity could go to the theatre on her own and not develop the friendships she says she wants.

Counsellor: I'm not sure how this will put you in touch with others?
Felicity: I'm not sure either. It's something I'd like to do though; and I don't go to the theatre, because I don't have anyone to go with.
Counsellor: I was wondering about theatre groups or evening classes which met for that purpose.

Felicity decides she will find out what evening classes or theatre groups there are in her area which would help to make theatre going a more social occasion.

You might use questions which focus on different degrees of success. For example, you might ask: 'If I were coping with this issue a little better I would be . . .'; 'If I were coping with this problem much better, I would be . . .'.

So far in this section on goal setting, we have considered several techniques for helping clients *identify* options or goals. Before considering what might be involved in planning action to achieve one or more of them, clients need to be helped to *evaluate* them in order to be able to make an informed decision.

Helping clients to appraise goals and decide which to opt for: force-field analysis.   Clients may favour some options over others and have greater chance of success with some than others. One valuable technique for appraising both goals and action plans is that of force-field analysis (Lewin, 1969). Let us look at what is involved.

Each of us occupies a 'life-space' which encompasses our physical surroundings, the community and family ties that we have, as well as aspects of ourselves as people – interests, values, strengths, achievements. Peoples' life-spaces are bounded by their physical, emotional and cognitive horizons. One way of viewing a 'life-space' is to see it as a battle ground in which various forces are operating. Some of the forces will be positive and will help them towards their goals. Some will be negative and inhibit their success. If clients want to achieve change, one way of assessing the feasibility of any change or goal is to ascertain which things in their 'life-spaces' will be positive and help them to achieve what they want and which will inhibit their progress, or go against them. Perhaps the best way to illustrate the technique is to give a specific example.

Deirdre's goal is to obtain a degree in Business Studies by full-time study, starting next academic year. She has the required entry qualifications but is finding it hard to make the decision. Her goal is clear, specific and within her resources. She lists all the things which would facilitate her achievement of that goal and all the things that would prevent or inhibit her. Thus:

Positives	*Negatives*
– fulfil an ambition	– spouse is not supportive
– leave a boring job	– anxiety that I'll fail
– time for study and spouse	– less personal money
– some savings to supplement income	– job is secure and well paid
	– life is settled

Positives	*Negatives*
– skills which can get me part-time work	– change is disruptive
– friends supportive	
– spouse has a well paid job	
– use qualifications	
– determination	

When recording what clients say, use their words. Continue by exploring each positive and negative force. Ask clients to expand on and discuss the implications of each force. Some counsellors ask clients to rate statements or to rank order them in order of importance. For example, Deirdre said that lack of support from her husband was the most inhibiting force on her list and the one which would be the most difficult one to overcome.

You will need your exploration and challenging skills to help clients to appraise their lists. For example, Deirdre's counsellor asked her precisely what she meant when she said her husband was unsupportive. Is it another way of saying that he is highly concerned that she will change and decide to leave him? Reviewing her list, Deirdre may decide that the negatives far outweigh the positives and this goal is not for her. She can then move on and look at some other options, such as part-time training or distance learning.

Using force-field analysis is an excellent way of encouraging clients to see themselves in context. It reminds both client and counsellor alike that we do not live in a vacuum and we are not omniscient. Family ties and obligations, social and community pressures may all operate either for or against us. It is not the length of the lists of positives and negatives that is important but the weight that clients attach to each force. You will sometimes need to challenge clients to reassess their lists and, for instance, explore whether or not a force is really so negative. Thus, when Deirdre says that change is disruptive, her counsellor might offer her the view that change can also be exciting, energising and stretching.

Force-field analysis should be a collaborative process. You may also wish to introduce aspects of your own, which you think that clients are overlooking. For example, some clients may say that they do not have the determination to sustain change. You may choose to point out times when they seem to have shown 'grit' in the past and ask them what is different now. Exploration and challenging will encourage clients to look afresh at what they have identified and the weightings they have allocated.

Here are some guidelines for using force-field analysis:

1   brainstorm-facilitating forces – those which will help clients reach their goals;
2   brainstorm-inhibiting forces – those which will prevent clients from reaching their goals;
3   check that the positives and negatives are 'real' and not 'assumed';
4   review what clients can do to maximise the positive forces and minimise the negative forces;
5   decide on the feasibility of the goal.

If clients are to succeed in achieving the change they want, they need to be committed to the options that they have chosen. Using force-field analysis will help clients to assess goals for their chances of success.

I want to discuss briefly a couple of difficulties often encountered in goal setting.

The goal is too large   Clients may want to make substantial changes in their lives and may know clearly what they want to achieve. However, viewed all at once, the change seems daunting. Clients will need help to break down a large goal into a series of smaller ones which provide a clear focus for action. Achieving small goals can boost confidence and may provide clients with the impetus to sustain their commitment to change.

Clients may also need to prioritise which goals to attempt first. For example, a client who has never had a close romantic/sexual relationship may need to develop his social skills before he risks approaching others. He may be being unrealistic in thinking that creating opportunities for meeting others is all he needs to do. He may not have good enough social skills to engage others whom he meets and he may become de-motivated by his lack of success at making new relationships.

Clients who do not want to set goals   Some clients, by the very act of recounting their concerns, will see clearly what they want to achieve and what they can do to achieve it. Other clients may be reluctant to commit themselves to change. If this occurs, you have several options:

1   go back to your contract and remind them what they said they wanted to gain for themselves in counselling. You may need to renegotiate the contract;
2   raise the issue and challenge them to examine their resistance to change;
3   ask them what benefits they are getting from their investment in counselling, if they are not changing in the ways which they

have said they wanted. Counselling is expensive in terms of effort and money. They may need to consider what pay-offs they are getting from their investment.

Change can be both liberating and frightening and you will need to be sensitive to this. However, supporting and challenging clients while they decide on what they want to accomplish is different from colluding with clients while they engage in fruitless exploration or debate.

To summarise, goal setting is an excellent strategy for:

1   identifying and focussing on what clients want to achieve;
2   helping clients to focus their attention and to mobilise their resources;
3   acting as a restraint against premature action (although some clients may need to act in order to discover what they want).

In order to be viable, goals should meet several criteria. They should be:

1   wanted by clients;
2   within the clients' resources;
3   clear and precisely outlining what the client will accomplish;
4   spelling out what clients will be doing differently and what others will see them doing;
5   set within a reasonable and specific period of time;
6   able to contribute in a significant way to handling clients' concerns.

Clients will be more likely to shape successful goals if they choose from a range of possible options. Three of the ways in which clients can be helped to generate goals are: imagining better futures; brainstorming; sentence completion.

Vague ideas for change need to be tailored to feasible goals. Force-field analysis can be used to help clients to: assess the feasibility of the goals they have identified; choose the options they will go for.

Goal setting requires continued exploration and challenging, if clients are to develop realistic options. Before taking any action, clients should be: clear about what it is they want to achieve; committed to their goals.

Let us now consider taking action.

Planning and taking action
Once clients have decided what goals they want to achieve, they will need to consider how they will achieve them. The first step in planning action is to help them to identify as many options for

action as possible. Again, brainstorming is a useful technique whereby you can collaborate in producing options for action. Clients may fail to change because they remain trapped in their limited options for action.

Consider the following example.

A client, Hannah, sought counselling because in her own words she 'felt awful' about herself. Her self-esteem was low, she saw herself as an unattractive woman whom no one would want to approach. Her self-evaluation prevented her from being close to others, taking opportunities which were presented both socially and at work. Hannah decided that one of the ways she could feel more confident about herself would be to lose some weight and become fitter. Her counsellor asked her how she would achieve her weight loss. She replied:

> *Hannah*: [*with a look of distaste*] I thought I'd go on the diet I read about in a magazine; or maybe join a slimming club. That's about it really.
> *Counsellor*: Those are two options. Any others you can think of?
> *Hannah*: There's only one way to lose weight, isn't there? Stop eating so much. More deprivation!
> *Counsellor*: I wonder whether we could explore ways in which you could change your eating without the rigid diet which you seem to dislike? We could also explore how deprived you believe you'll be.
> *Hannah*: I would so like to feel comfortable with myself and not be governed by what I can and can't eat. What do I need to do?
> *Counsellor*: I suggest that we list all the ways that we can think of that might help you to lose weight. You can be as creative as you like. Once we have a list of options, we can review it and decide which ones appeal to you.

Here is Hannah's original list:

- go to a health farm to get a good start
- join a slimming club
- have my jaw wired
- take slimming pills
- take exercise like swimming
- fast one day per week
- eat what I like but give up alcohol
- take up smoking
- monitor myself and only eat when I'm hungry

Hannah reviewed her list and rejected wiring her jaw, taking slimming pills and smoking because they were not in keeping with her values; giving up alcohol because she drank very little and enjoyed it – she didn't want more deprivation; the slimming club because it would be repeating old patterns and increase her feelings of deprivation.

The following options were considered possible:

- taking exercise
- monitoring herself and eating only when hungry
- fasting one day each week
- going to a health farm

Hannah decided that she would try monitoring herself and taking exercise. Her counsellor offered her the notion of allowing her body to tell her when it was hungry and needed food. Together they worked out a plan of diary keeping and Hannah agreed that she would record the times when she noticed she felt hungry and her accompanying feelings and thoughts on these occasions. Her counsellor also raised the notion of exercise, such as dance or yoga, which would help her to become more in touch with her body. In the process of identifying possible action steps, her counsellor challenged Hannah to explore what being hungry meant to her. She attended to Hannah's feelings and confronted her view that there is only one way to tackle this problem.

The process of identifying and choosing suitable action plans demands that you continue to explore with and challenge clients. Some clients may avoid certain possibilities for action because of their largely untested beliefs. For example, they may fear rejection or believe that they will be thought of as rude. Others may be responding to outdated 'shoulds' and 'oughts' which do not reflect their current reality.

You may need to explore with clients how they will stop themselves from taking action. Once clients know how they stop themselves, it is harder for them to keep doing it. The way is then open to discuss how they can halt their attempts to undermine their plans. For example, a client who says that he tells himself 'You'll fail. You won't succeed' can be helped, among other things, to identify positive messages to replace the negative ones.

There are various techniques for helping clients to choose what action out of the many possibilities to take. I have already discussed force-field analysis (in the previous section) as a technique for assessing goals: it can also be used to assess the probable success or failure of action plans. Balance sheets are useful for reviewing the costs/benefits and probability of success of any action. If clients are aware of obstacles, they will be in a better position either to find ways of overcoming them or to look at other options which will not meet the same degree of opposition.

What stops clients from acting
1 *They do not have the skills*. It may be unwise to encourage a

person who has been unemployed for a long time to start going for interviews. Such a client may need to take a short course in self-presentation or interview skills first.

2   *There are risks involved.* These might be real or imagined. I have touched on this in the previous section and I think it is important that clients explore their fears and beliefs about possible risks. Some clients may discover that they need information; others may realise that the risks they imagine do not belong to this situation at all. Risks can also be graded from 'High to Low'.

3   *There are constraints involved.* Clients do have real constraints in their lives and it is important that these are recognised and explored. However, they may also imagine constraints.

4   *The rewards are not perceived as great enough.* Part of the action planning process is to help clients identify and create a reward system for themselves. You will need to help clients to decide whether the pay-offs for taking risks are ample enough for them.

5   *Clients want a perfect action plan.* There is, of course, no such thing. All change carries some risks and no plan is fail safe. Clients can be helped both to identify risks and to discover options for minimising them.

Consider the following example. A client, Lucy, is talking about her five year old daughter.

Lucy: I want to be absolutely sure that I'm doing the right thing. I don't want her to become a delinquent or a drop-out. The early years are important, aren't they?
Counsellor: I admire your concern and I think you're telling me that you must have certainty.
Lucy: I do . . . and that's not possible, is it? I want to do my best though.
Counsellor: Let's talk through what action you think would be the most successful.

Taking action   In order to take and to sustain action, clients might need to do the following:

1   *Identify a suitable reward system.* By 'suitable', I mean one that fits clients' values, is both adequate and realistic and does not undermine the action plan. For example, a client who wishes to control his drinking would not be advised to reward himself with a wine-tasting event!

Rewards help clients both to get started and to maintain their commitment. You may reward clients by noticing changes they make and by praising new and positive behaviour. Logs and diaries can be helpful as 'progress charts'. A record of achievement is often rewarding for clients when the going gets tough.

One client was encouraged to record all the positive comments she received each week. She found it much harder to dismiss herself as stupid when faced with a list of compliments.

2 *Establish a support system.* If you are the client's only support, then you will need to raise this as an issue. The support of friends, family and colleagues can be important for any client who wants to change. Support systems give encouragement by providing both rewards and practical help. They may also provide opportunities for sharing information and concerns which decrease clients' sense of isolation. It is not uncommon for clients to feel anxious when trying out new things for the first time. It is possible too that they may experience a decrease in enthusiasm for sticking to their action plan. Exploring with them what and who can help them when they feel anxious or when they feel like giving up may help to sustain them. You may also discuss with them what support and encouragement they would like from you.

Evaluating and sustaining change

The question you will need to address with clients is 'Is the problem being resolved by this action?' If it is, then you and the client may consider ending the counselling. If not, then you will need to explore what is happening for the client. Sometimes taking action helps clients to see that the problem that they brought masks another deeper issue. Also, the goals that clients set may be inappropriate and need to be reassessed. Finally, clients sometimes fail to achieve what they want because they time their action inappropriately. For example, the client who tries to discuss his relationship with his wife when she is putting their children to bed. Timing is often crucial to successful action.

Helping clients to secure their future by sustaining the changes they have made is generally a feature of the Ending Stage. Marx (1984) has outlined a number of considerations important to sustaining change and avoiding relapses into old and unhelpful behaviour patterns. In addition to establishing a support system, you might help clients to:

1 *Identify situations in which they are most likely to revert to their old behaviours.* For example, it may be under stress at work or during weekends when they are on their own. If they can identify times, places or people with whom they are likely to compromise their new behaviour, they can avoid these situations when they are feeling vulnerable.
2 *Identify environments which support the 'old' behaviour and*

avoid them. For example, a client who wishes to stop smoking may find it more difficult, if she continues to socialise in pubs with her friends and where smoking is an enjoyable accompaniment to drinking.

3 *Observe and learn emotional control*. Clients may feel anxious when they experience a challenge to their new behaviour. They may believe they will go out of control or that they will be humiliated. If clients can learn to identify their feelings (and the beliefs which accompany them), they will be in a position to control them and remain 'in charge'.

Consider the following example. Alice sought counselling because at times she behaved ineffectually at work. She described herself as 'powerless' and 'losing all her social skills'. In the Beginning and Middle Stages, Alice learned that her powerlessness was a defence against possible attack. She feared criticism, because it was redolent of the disgrace she experienced as a child. Alice set goals to become more assertive and to control her fear. She explored what would happen, if she faced criticism after she had expressed her views.

> *Alice*: Sometimes I'm aware of feeling frightened. I'm aware of the urge to withdraw and to protect myself. When I feel this way I say to myself, 'Stop and listen to others. You are competent and they can't destroy you. It's alright for people to disagree with you and that doesn't make you wrong or stupid.' That helps me to see what is *really* going on, rather than what I create.

4 *Create a system of internal rewards*. Self-praise coupled with knowledge of results can be powerful in helping clients to sustain their new behaviour. Recording, for example, their assertiveness, weight loss, abstinence from alcohol or cigarettes can provide a rewarding feedback system. If clients are hesitant to do this, ask them to keep a record for a trial period of two weeks.

Ending

Endings are an important part of the counselling process and may be concerned with loss as well as with celebration of achievements. Let us consider some of the issues in ending.

When to end Counselling is a contractual relationship and the ending usually occurs when clients have achieved what they set out to achieve or when they are coping sufficiently well with their concerns to need no further assistance. For example, one client remarked:

I feel much happier about saying what I think to my partner and I know I'm using my skills at work to be more direct with colleagues. I'm also aware that I could be more direct with my boss, I'm not handling that as well as I'd like but I'm satisfied with what I've achieved. So, I think I'll finish now.

Planning to end   One of the distinguishing characteristics of the counselling relationship is its temporary nature. From the outset, all the work which clients undertake moves them towards the time when they will no longer have the need or wish for counselling support. Of course, you will need to remind clients of the number of contracted sessions you have left together. You might say something like: 'I'm aware that we have this and one further session of the six we originally contracted for. I'd like us to review how far you've got towards achieving what you wanted and to discuss options for further sessions, if you want them.'

You will need to plan your ending. The end of counselling will be signalled by clients achieving what they wanted. However, you will need to leave adequate time for them to identify, explore and express their feelings about the ending and the loss of the relationship. Clients will have spent time in your company revealing more of their secret fears and hopes than possibly at any previous time in their lives. You will have 'held' them when they have expressed intense feelings and been witness to the side of themselves which they have found unacceptable. The ending of the counselling relationship may resonate with other painful endings which they have experienced and perhaps never resolved.

Consider the following example. Ken, the client, is a young man who has decided to finish counselling.

> *Counsellor*: Next week will be our last session and I was wondering what thoughts and feelings you have about that?
>
> *Ken*: Not much really. [*Looking at his feet*] If it's ending, that's it, isn't it?
>
> *Counsellor*: [*playing a hunch*] I wonder what usually happens in endings in your life?
>
> *Ken*: [*looking bright*] Nothing, because I avoid them!
>
> *Counsellor*: I shall miss seeing you.
>
> *Ken*: [*in tears*] This is why I avoid them. I get sad.

The counsellor encouraged Ken to express his sadness. They explored the ending of their relationship. Ken made a connection between dismissing the importance of the ending with his counselling contract. At the start of counselling he had a poor self-image and low self-esteem. His wish to avoid focussing on the ending had to do with his old belief that he was too insignificant to be missed and he had therefore decided not to miss others.

Alerting clients to the possibility of feelings of sadness and loss
Clients may not expect to experience painful feelings at the close of
a counselling relationship. However, alerting them to the possibility
can be a way of both giving them permission and of preparing them
for what may occur. I am not suggesting that clients *ought* to feel
sad and that something is amiss if they do not; rather that some
clients, particularly those who have difficulty expressing feelings,
may feel freer to express what feelings they do have, if the issue is
raised with them. You might say something like:

> *Counsellor*: I'm aware that we haven't talked about how you're feeling.
> *Client*: I feel OK. It seems the right thing to do. I'm much more
> confident now; and I'm developing new friendships and life seems
> much freer.
> *Counsellor*: You sound much stronger. I also wondered if there was any
> sadness for you in this ending?
> *Client*: I'm not aware of feeling sad, [*pause*] although it will seem really
> strange not coming here any more.

Being open to negative feelings   Not all counselling relationships
end when clients have completed the work of their contracts. Some
clients will end prematurely in your view, because they believe you
are not helping them. It is not possible to help every client who
walks through the door and some will resist your efforts, no matter
how skilful you are being. Counsellors also make mistakes. You
can but do your best with the skills and knowledge that you have
and ensure that you have good supervision to support your work.
However, it is sometimes hard to receive negative feedback from
clients about their experience of counselling with you. The following guidelines may assist you at such times:

1   offer to support clients in their search for another counsellor. It
    may be that they would benefit from working with someone else
    who has a different style and approach;
2   use your reflective skills to accept their disappointment or anger;
3   give feedback about how you feel in a non-judgemental way;
4   describe concretely what you think has happened and own your
    part in it. However, I do not mean that you take responsibility
    for clients' failure to commit themselves to change;
5   respect their right to do what they want to do. You may think
    that they have more work to do and would not advise finishing
    at this juncture. However, clients have the right to look else-
    where and to decide what is best for them;
6   if appropriate, review what you think have been the positive
    steps they have taken in their work with you.

Review the learning Endings provide an opportunity for clients to review their learning and their development. Encourage participation in the review to ensure that it does not become like a test. Ward (1984) has suggested the following guidelines for helping clients both to focus and to reflect on the journey they have taken with you:

1 Ask them to think back to how they were at the beginning of counselling and to compare what they are doing differently now. Relate their new behaviours to the contracts they made with you and encourage them to take credit for their achievements. Share your perception of how they have changed and developed. Make sure that the feedback you give is specific and focussed.
2 If you have taped your work you might want to play a piece of tape which demonstrates their new thinking or their new insights.
3 Share and discuss what have been the critical or important times in the counselling sessions.
4 Look to the future and spend some time discussing how they will use their new behaviour to tackle other related issues or anticipated problems.

Summary

The Ending Stage typically has action and closure as its foci.

Goals are developed from the new insights gained through the process of challenging. They are 'what' clients wish to achieve; in other words, the outcomes they value and regard as important for coping with their concerns.

To be viable, goals should be within clients' resources and specify clearly what the outcome will be.

Action plans are based on the goals which the client has chosen. They identify precisely how clients will achieve their goals.

Ending the counselling relationship will usually occur when clients have achieved their stated goals. Consideration needs to be given to the end of the relationship and the significance of that for clients.

6   Case-study

The subject of this case-study is a client called Gerry. The following information, gained over the first two sessions, is presented here to provide a context for the counselling. This case-study represents the work of ten sessions. I have highlighted and described what I consider the salient aspects in terms of the model discussed in this book. I also include the reflections made by the counsellor in between sessions and her tentative session plans.

Gerry is 29 years old. He left school at the age of 18 after taking three A levels. He passed two and failed one. He has had a variety of jobs since he left school, for example, care assistant with the elderly, a short spell of work in a large psychiatric hospital, sales trainee with a local store and van driving. At present, he is doing clerical work for an agency. His partner of two years, Anna, has just finished her training as an occupational therapist and works in a large local hospital. Gerry decided to seek counselling because he has felt increasingly moody and irritable over the last six to nine months. He and Anna have been fighting more frequently and he feels very distressed about this. Anna had done a counselling workshop recently and, during one of their fights, had angrily suggested that 'he get some counselling and sort himself out'.

He made his initial contact over the telephone. The counsellor asked him briefly what issues he wanted to deal with and offered information about the way she worked. Gerry told her that he was feeling depressed and had a 'relationship problem'. She specifically asked him if there was anything he would like to check with her. They made one appointment for an assessment session. The counsellor explained that she would like both of them to have the opportunity to get to know each other a little better before deciding whether or not to work together.

Session 1

The counsellor's primary aim in this session was to begin to build a counselling relationship with Gerry. She was concerned to listen and to respond with understanding to both how he saw himself and his concerns. In order to do this, she made considerable use of both paraphrasing and statements. She followed his lead and encouraged him to say what was important for him. However, throughout the session she listened for patterns and themes and formulated tentative hypotheses.

Counsellor: Hello Gerry, please sit down [*indicates a chair*].

Gerry: Thank you. [*He looks directly at the counsellor and smiles. She notices that he is tapping his fingers on his legs. She wonders what he is feeling. She decides to take the lead and encourage him to begin.*]

Counsellor: You told me over the telephone that you've been feeling depressed recently and that you're concerned about your relationship with your partner.

Gerry: Yes, that's right but I'm not sure where to begin really. I had it all planned out before I came and now I don't know where to start. My mind's all mixed up. I was thinking my life's all mixed up. Sometimes I don't think there's anything right in it. Perhaps, if there's anything you'd like to know about me, any questions you'd like to ask me!

Counsellor: [*nodding*] I'm wondering what's uppermost in your mind now. [*Counsellor resists the invitation from Gerry to set a pattern of asking questions which might control the direction of the session. However, she wants to help him to begin. She uses a statement to encourage him to say more.*]

Gerry: [*with a wry smile*] Well, the mood swings. And it's got much worse over the last six months or so. I wake up some mornings and I feel terrible. I don't understand it. I tell myself that I'm being ridiculous and I should just snap out of it, that life isn't so bad. I ought not to be like this. That's why I'm here I suppose.

Counsellor: You're feeling miserable more of the time and blaming yourself [*paraphrase focussing on feeling*].

Gerry: Yes, I wait and wonder what will hit me. I've always been called moody, but just lately I have been feeling depressed more and more of the time. I wake up in the morning and wonder what sort of day I'm going to have. That may sound daft, but I can't point to anything that's happened and say 'well, I feel like this because of such and such'. I can't understand what's happening to me. The more I try to be happy, the worse it is. Yesterday morning I thought, 'I *will* have a good day', but by lunchtime I felt dreadful.

Counsellor: It sounds like you see yourself at the mercy of your feelings. You can't control them or make sense of what's happening to you. Is that it? [*Counsellor uses a paraphrase both to check and to show understanding.*]

Gerry: Yes, and I hate feeling like that.

Counsellor: Like . . . ?

Gerry: Oh! defeated, at rock bottom, not wanting to be bothered with anyone. Sad and just wanting to get away from everything and everyone. I don't think Anna will put up with me for much longer, if I go on like this. It's not much fun for her.

Counsellor: Or for you, I would imagine. You sound weary and unhappy. [*She wants to keep the focus on Gerry and to recognise how he feels.*]

The counsellor wonders who has called Gerry 'moody' but decides not to ask him at this point. She thinks the question will divert him to a discussion of others and she wants to encourage him to talk about himself. Gerry goes on to say how he is scared he will drive Anna away. He talks about his relationship, saying that, although Anna is independent and has a career of her own, she relies on him for support. The counsellor noticed that he sounded rather resentful when he said that. He says that he loves her but is not sure of her feelings for him and her commitment to him. Since they have been together, she has become increasingly involved with her course and her new job. He has shouldered much of the domestic work, for example cleaning and shopping at the weekends. He is proud of her success and adds that her enthusiasm for her work is 'a bit much' sometimes.

> *Counsellor*: A bit much. [*Reflects to encourage Gerry to be more concrete.*]
>
> *Gerry*: Yes, she talks a lot about it and keeps asking me what I think about what she's doing. She talks about people I don't know and who don't mean anything to me. I'm pleased she's keen and got a job she really likes but sometimes . . . well! you know how it is? [*shrugs his shoulders*]
>
> *Counsellor*: You find her enthusiasm hard to face when you're feeling so miserable, is that it? [*She decides to challenge Gerry by stating what he has implied, even though it is early on in the relationship.*]
>
> *Gerry*: Yeah! It's like I'm having my nose rubbed in it. She doesn't realise what it's like being without the sort of job you want, and wondering if you'll ever get it. I'm still doing boring clerical work. I can't see much of a career for myself in that or much satisfaction. You can't play around for ever, can you.
>
> *Counsellor*: You sound pessimistic about your future. I'm not sure how you've been 'playing around' up to now. [*Counsellor paraphrases and ends with a statement to encourage him to be more concrete.*]

Gerry agrees that he is pessimistic. He explains how he has shifted from job to job, in an effort to find one that he really likes. He wonders whether he will ever find work that stretches him and provides variety and stimulation. He talks as if there is something wrong with him and dismisses himself with phrases like, 'I'm fickle' and 'I've got a grasshopper mentality'. He says he *should* have a career. It is what his family want for him and what he wants for himself. He describes his older sister as a disappointment to his parents. The counsellor decides not pursue the lead about his sister at present, wanting to keep the focus on Gerry. She notices that he is looking unhappy as he talks and as the following dialogue shows, she invites him to focus on how he feels.

> *Counsellor*: You seem sad now as you talk. [*paraphrase to help Gerry to express what he is feeling now*]

Gerry: I am, because I just can't imagine myself being that lucky. You feel so useless a lot of the time, like you've let everyone down. I haven't made anything of myself. At school, I had potential but that was ten years ago and what do I have to show for it? And the waste of it all too.

The counsellor notices how he uses words which distance the problem from himself, for example 'it' and 'you'. He also hints that what happens to him will be a matter of luck. Her hunch is that he believes that he can have little influence over his future and that 'unworthy people' do not get what they want. She decides to log these ideas for the present. She responds by focussing on Gerry and using 'you'.

Counsellor: You've been reviewing your life and telling yourself that you're useless and that you've let your parents down. Sounds like a painful conclusion.

Gerry: Yes it is. I see other friends who are settled with jobs and partners. I know that my parents would like grandchildren and I feel that I'm not giving them what they want. Also, I haven't got a job I like. I've been left behind in the race. Some of the people from my year at school are doing much better than me and I wonder how come they find it so easy to find work and settle down and I just can't manage it. That's how it feels, most of the time. Perhaps [*with a laugh*] my life story would make a good soap opera! I like the idea of that.

At this point, Gerry switches to humour and does not continue to express his sadness and frustration. She thinks that he is defending against misery by using humour. She decides that it is too premature to share her hunch. However, she wants to let Gerry know what she has observed and give him the opportunity to explore how he uses humour. The following short section demonstrates this.

Counsellor: I notice that you ended what you were saying with a joke about yourself. [*Counsellor makes a statement encouraging Gerry to focus on his behaviour. He brushes it aside.*]

Gerry: I like a good laugh and my sense of humour keeps me going. I can usually see the funny side of things.

Counsellor: Joking about yourself when you feel disappointed or miserable helps you to cope. [*The counsellor decides to paraphrase what Gerry has said. She thinks that in future sessions she will need to invite him to explore how he uses humour to dismiss painful feelings. He is not ready to reveal to her how hurt he is at present.*]

The session has fifteen minutes left to run and the counsellor decides to signal the ending and move towards a contract.

Counsellor: We have fifteen minutes left and I wonder how you're feeling now that you have told me something of your concerns.

Gerry: Fine . . . I imagined lots of things before I came here, like you'd laugh or something. I'm relieved that you didn't and I'm surprised at how much I've said. I've said some things that I don't often admit to, like feeling useless and sad.

Counsellor: I'm pleased you've said something of what's on your mind. I'm aware that we haven't specifically talked about what you want to achieve for yourself – what you want to change as a result of counselling.

Gerry: I don't want to be so miserable and feel so awful about myself. I suppose I want what most people want and that's to be happier.

Counsellor: And if you were happier, what would be going on in your life? [*invites a contrast*]

Gerry: I'd have a job I liked and I'd be feeling better about myself.

Counsellor: Feeling better about yourself means. [*Counsellor invites Gerry to be more concrete.*]

Gerry: I'd feel more secure. I'd feel more equal and successful. I wouldn't feel so anxious about losing Anna either.

Counsellor: And your thoughts about counselling and working with me?

Gerry: Fine. How long do you think I'll need?

Counsellor: I suggest that we contract for six sessions and then a review with the option of further sessions, if you want them. How does that sound?

Gerry: That's fine with me.

The counsellor confirms her fee and raises the issue of payment for cancelled sessions by saying:

Counsellor: I will normally charge you for sessions which you cancel with less than a week's notice.

As the session ends and Gerry gets up to leave the room, he says:

Gerry: I expect you have lots of miserable people like me. Don't you get bored with other people's problems?

The counsellor makes the following hypotheses:

- Gerry is seeking reassurance that he is not boring.
- He wants to feel special to the counsellor and not one of a number of miserable people.
- He wants reassurance that his concerns are not unique and that other clients have similar problems.
- He wants to know if the counsellor has the expertise to work with someone like him.

She decides on the basis of what Gerry has disclosed to treat his question as a plea for her understanding and acceptance. She replies:

Counsellor: I have been interested in what you've shared with me today.

I think we can work together and that you will be able to make the changes you want.

After the first session, the counsellor reviewed what Gerry had told her. Using the framework Work, Relationships, Identity (see Chapter 2), she made the following assessments.

Identity

She thought that this was the main issue for Gerry. He does not appear to value himself or believe he is a 'worthwhile' person. The counsellor's hunch was that his low self-esteem inhibits him from seeking work or training which would stretch and develop him. His lack of self-concern was crucial to the development of the other areas of his life. She also noted his age and wondered if his impending thirtieth birthday was the catalyst in his wish both to review what he had achieved so far and to secure a more satisfying future.

Relationships

With others   She hypothesised that he may not have enough self-regard to seek equality in his relationship with Anna and that he believes he does not deserve to get what he wants. She also thought that Gerry might feel competitive with Anna. His misery and mood swings were perhaps based not only on his insecurity in his relationship and fear of rejection but also on the fact that Anna seemed to be succeeding where he was not. He did not volunteer information about other friendships. The counsellor gained some information about his immediate family and their expectations of him.

With the counsellor   In his reactions to her, the counsellor noticed that Gerry made a joke about his painful feelings and did not show anger when he talked about his differences with Anna. She wondered if he would be compliant with her and refrain from saying what he felt or thought if it conflicted with her ideas. She believed that their relationship would be important because, if Gerry learned to trust her – to believe that he was valued and accepted by her – he would then begin to value himself.

Work

Gerry was dissatisfied in his current job. The counsellor realised that she had little information about how he spent his leisure time.

The counsellor decided that, in the next session, she would encourage him to explore further his belief that he was lacking in worth and invite him to express his sadness and resentment. She would continue to listen for clues which either supported or disconfirmed her initial assessments. Finally, she would listen for openings to raise a discussion of family/other relationships.

Session 2

The counsellor decides to open with a 'choice-point summary' (as described in Chapter 3) both to check her understanding of the previous session and to bring them both to a common starting point.

> *Counsellor*: Gerry, last week we discussed how you feel about yourself. We also talked about your relationship with Anna and your boredom with your current job, I wonder whether you would like to continue with one of those concerns or are there other issues you would like to talk about. [*Counsellor does not want to set the agenda for the session.*]
>
> *Gerry*: I've actually had a much calmer week. It's hard to explain but I've felt more hopeful about life. Anna and I haven't fought so much, so that's a relief. Work is still awful though. I realised that when I talk about it how bored and dissatisfied I am. It's like, if I don't say anything, I don't have to face what a grim work life I have.
>
> *Counsellor*: I'm pleased you've been feeling more relaxed. It sounds like the work issue is in the forefront today.
>
> *Gerry*: I don't want to stay in this job. I've got the day off today and, when I woke up this morning, I felt so relieved.

Gerry continues in an energetic way after this exchange. He says that he wants more from life and thinks he has more to offer. She notices that he seems to hold contradictory views of himself, for example being 'useless' and having something to offer. The counsellor decides to encourage Gerry further. She believes that he maintains a position of himself as unworthy by overlooking or denying his abilities and strengths. What happens next is the counsellor beginning to challenge Gerry's self-evaluation. As I described in Chapter 4, challenging involves helping clients to reassess their concerns through deeper exploration.

> *Counsellor*: I'm wondering what you have to offer in a job. [*The counsellor uses a statement. She decides against a direct question such as 'What do you have to offer?' She also wants to encourage him to begin to be more specific. If Gerry is eventually to set goals and take action, he must have a clear idea what his strengths and resources are.*]
>
> *Gerry*: [thoughtfully] This is hard. It's like boasting. I don't know really.
>
> *Counsellor*: You're embarrassed saying positive things about yourself.
>
> *Gerry*: [smiling] Yes I am a bit! I don't know, depends on what you mean by strengths and abilities, doesn't it?

The counsellor thinks this is an invitation to discussion, so that Gerry can distance himself from the issue and avoid talking about himself in a positive way. The counsellor presses him gently.

Counsellor: What would a close friend say about your abilities, Gerry?

Gerry: [*thinking*] Well, I'm reliable and I can work hard. I'm a good listener and I'm intelligent. I failed an A level, because I hated school and messed around. I regret that now. What else . . . I care about others and I'm efficient. Most of the jobs I've had have been easy to get the hang of. I'm usually told that I've done well in them. That's about it.

Counsellor: That doesn't seem like a portrait of a 'useless' person to me. [*Counsellor offers her perspective to challenge Gerry.*]

Gerry: No, I don't suppose it does. But that is how I feel – 'worthless', 'useless'.

Counsellor: That's what you believe about yourself. Put some feelings to that belief, Gerry. [*The counsellor gives Gerry a directive. She also distinguishes between the beliefs Gerry has about himself (see Chapter 4) and encourages him to express what feelings may be attached to that belief.*]

Gerry: I feel sad and ashamed I suppose. I've let people down.

Counsellor: I wonder who has been let down by you.

Gerry talks about his family's expectations of him. He says that his parents never expressed a clear preference about what they wanted for him. However, he knew that they wanted him 'to succeed'. He explained that his elder sister left school after her A levels and married a year later. His parents were disappointed, because she refused higher education and they disliked her husband. Gerry reveals that his sister has just separated from her husband and his parents are very worried. He emphasises that she has always caused them concern and says that they have pinned their hopes on him.

Counsellor: You're to make amends for your sister's behaviour. You sound angry.

Gerry: Yes I am. She's always done exactly as she wanted – always been selfish. I'm left picking up the pieces.

Counsellor: Doing what you want is selfish then, is it? [*Challenges by pointing to the conclusions of what Gerry is saying.*]

Gerry: [*looking uncomfortable*] Yes, I mean No! I don't suppose it is. It's what I think about her though, so I suppose I do see it like that.

Counsellor: If you don't do what your parents expect and make amends you're being selfish.

What is happening here is the counsellor beginning to challenge Gerry to explore his belief that doing what he wants is selfish. He begins to see that deciding what he wants does not mean acting irresponsibly or hurtfully towards others. Gerry also realises that he is neither sure of what he wants for himself, nor does he have a clear idea of what his parents expect of him. The session ends with Gerry looking thoughtful.

In this session, the counsellor challenged Gerry's self-evaluation. When she confronted him to identify his strengths, her intention was to help him see himself in a more realistic and therefore more favourable light. The counsellor was tentative, but wondered if she offered too many challenges to Gerry's frame of reference.

Session 3

The counsellor prepares to explore any negative feelings that Gerry may have had after the previous session. However, he begins to talk about feeling 'freer'. He realised painfully after the last session how much his sense of worth is dependent on the approval of others.

He says that he is thinking seriously about changing jobs and would like to start with that. He looked through the newspapers at job advertisements and identified two that interested him. He has sent for the application forms. He is talking with less enthusiasm now. The counsellor decides to check what she is picking up and to share what she has noticed about the jobs he has mentioned.

> *Counsellor*: Both jobs seem of a similar level and type to the work you have now. Last week, you told me that you wanted a career, an interesting job which would stretch you. You don't sound enthusiastic to me. [*She challenges Gerry by pointing to an apparent contradiction. Her intention is to encourage him to begin to explore how he might be limiting himself.*]
>
> *Gerry*: I suppose they are. Without training, I guess that's the level I'll have to aim at. When I was at school, I wanted to do law. I gave up the idea, because I couldn't stand the thought of all that training, particularly after A levels. I'd had enough.
>
> *Counsellor*: And now? [*Uses a question as a prompt to encourage Gerry to talk about the present.*]
>
> Gerry: Now I wouldn't mind doing some training, but it's too late now, isn't it? Anyway, I don't have the qualifications. I haven't made a very good job at organising my life, have I?
>
> *Counsellor*: Whether or not it's too late for you to train depends on what you choose to do.
>
> *Gerry*: [*truculently*] I know that! I won't be able to get a job for which I'm not qualified, will I? That's obvious.
>
> *Counsellor*: You sound angry now [*Gerry nods*] and I wonder what happened when I answered you. [*Counsellor uses immediacy both to focus on what Gerry is feeling and to invite him to explore his reaction to her response. She also wanted to accept his feeling.*]
>
> *Gerry*: What happened? I don't know. I felt really angry and I don't understand it.
>
> *Counsellor*: And you thought?
>
> Gerry: It's OK for you! What do you know about failure and not having the sort of life that you want. I loathed school, couldn't wait to get out. You try coping at boarding school, being expected to like it, when you hate it. My parents said I could leave, if I wanted, but that would have been letting the side down. So I stayed and put up with

the teasing and the homesickness. You can get used to most things, you know.

Counsellor: When I said 'I guess it depends on what you choose to do', I wasn't recognising the lack of choice you once had and what little choice you think you have now.

The above dialogue demonstrates the use of *immediacy* as a challenging strategy. The counsellor focussed on how Gerry was responding to her, as a way of encouraging him to explore his beliefs.

Gerry returns to his past and reveals that he was sent to boarding-school at the age of 7 and all of his school career had been spent away from home. He hated school and was torn between wanting to leave and not wanting to disappoint his parents. While his parents said he could leave, if he wanted to, he sensed that they wanted him to stay. He remembered his mother's letters containing sympathy for him in his misery, and saying how sad she was that he was unhappy. Gerry wanted his parents to take the action which he could not and that was to remove him from school. He felt his misery was not 'heard' by them. His predicament was further intensified by the knowledge that his sister enjoyed boarding-school.

Gerry: My sister revelled in boarding-school, you know. She made friends, joined in and, looking back on it, seemed to prefer school to home. I hated it. I just got stuck into work for a time. It was one way of not feeling so awful, I suppose. I got teased as a swot too. Talking about it now, I couldn't seem to do anything right. I was such a failure [*with a weak smile*].

Counsellor: You coped at school, passed your O levels and went on to an A level course. You're talking about *yourself* as a failure. I think you're being hard on yourself and overlooking what you achieved. Does that make any sense? [*The counsellor challenges Gerry by giving her perspective. Her intention is to encourage him to look more realistically at what he achieved and to separate his evaluation of himself as a person from his evaluation of his behaviour.*]

Gerry: [*laughing sarcastically*] You mean it's alright to screw up my A levels.

Counsellor: [*in a serious voice*] I'm distinguishing between failing an exam and labelling yourself a failure. Sticking at something you didn't like for perhaps ten years and working hard for much of the time takes determination. I respect you for that and I don't think it's funny.

Gerry is silent for some minutes. He looks reflective and his response indicates that he has listened to and accepted the counsellor's challenge.

Gerry: I never thought of myself as determined. I didn't exactly 'grin and bear it' at school though, more like 'cry and bear it', but I didn't give up. I did well in my O levels too. I suppose A levels seemed the more important exams.

Counsellor: I don't want to dismiss the importance you've attached to A levels or your disappointment at your performance. I'm interested in how you might overlook your achievements and focus on failure. You also seem to be saying that it wasn't enough to remain at school, you should have liked it as well. That sounds like a tall order.

During the remainder of the session, Gerry explores some of his 'oughts' and 'shoulds'. He reveals that he believes that he 'ought' to like what his parents want for him and that he 'shouldn't' give up. The counsellor offers him the perspective that some of his 'oughts' and 'shoulds' may not serve him well in his adult life. Some may be outdated and restricting. He begins to see how he has tyrannised himself with the label 'useless'. The counsellor also reminds him that he can decide to act differently in the future.

Counsellor: As a child, you were reliant on your parents. You're an adult now and you do have the power to change.

During the past three sessions, the counsellor has concentrated on understanding how Gerry sees his concerns and encouraging him to explore his thoughts, feelings and behaviour. She has begun to challenge him to explore more deeply and believes, by the way he has received her challenges, that he is beginning to see himself and his relationships from a different perspective.

She thinks that the crucial challenges were those which enabled Gerry to distinguish between his past behaviour (hating school, failing an exam and a series of unsatisfying jobs) and his evaluation of himself as a person. She has also challenged his use of humour by not colluding with his laughter and saying clearly what she thinks.

The counselling work has moved between the Beginning Stage of initial exploration and the Middle Stage of making a reassessment. The counsellor thinks that Gerry trusts her enough to risk exploring the fundamental issue of his identity.

Session 4

The fourth session shows how in one session, it is possible to move from exploration through reassessment to goals and action. The session began with the counsellor commenting on Gerry's non-verbal behaviour. He looked tense and irritable.

Counsellor: You look tense, Gerry.

Gerry: Anna's going to a friend's for the weekend and it appears that I'm not invited. She's going without me. [*angrily*] She didn't think

that I might be disappointed or that she could have refused to go
without me.

Counsellor: You're angry because you've been left out. [*paraphrases to
show understanding.*]

Gerry: [*in a flat voice*] Yes, I am. I told her they were thoughtless. She
said that she didn't agree. That these friends don't know me, so why
should they invite me? I left it at that and I woke up this morning
feeling awful.

Counsellor: [*tentatively*] I'm not sure if you've told Anna how you feel
and asked her not to go and she's refused.

Gerry: No, it's obvious. She could tell that I was upset and I didn't want
her to go. Anyway what's the point in asking people who have
already made up their minds what they're going to do? Do I have to
ask for everything?

Gerry is behaving passively. He believes that Anna will know what
he wants and that he cannot influence her once she has made a
decision. She decides to challenge his views, as the following
dialogue shows.

Counsellor: [*gently*] Gerry, I can understand your hurt at being excluded. I don't want to sound harsh, but I wonder how Anna will know
what you want, if you don't tell her. Does that make any sense to
you?

Gerry: [*crossly*] What's the point? It won't do any good. She's going and
that's that. It's all very well saying, 'tell her how you feel and what
you want'! Why should I have to ask for everything? I'm supposed to
be her partner. Surely she should have some idea of what I feel and
what's important to me. [*looking sad*] You just don't understand. I
never do anything right here.

Counsellor: You look sad. [*focussing on what Gerry is feeling*]

Gerry: [*looking tearful*] I'm thinking about boarding-school. I wrote
saying I was unhappy and asked to leave. They wrote back saying
that I'm sure I would get used to it.

Counsellor: And you wanted them to come and take you away?

Gerry talks about school, remembering how frightened he felt on
leaving home. He expresses anger with his parents for their lack of
understanding and protection. The counsellor is aware that Gerry
is focussing on his past. When he came in to the session, he was
angry with Anna and hurt at her decision to spend the weekend
with friends.

Counsellor: Gerry, I wonder if you can make any connections between
what happened to you at school and what's happening now with
Anna? [*Challenges Gerry by inviting him to explore a possible pattern
in his life.*]

Gerry: You mean my parents didn't do what I wanted, so what's the
point in asking for anything now?

Counsellor: Asking doesn't pay, perhaps.

Gerry: Well, I don't feel I ought to ask her. She has the right to do what

she wants to do and to visit friends on her own, if she wants to. I
don't want to put pressure on her. [*Counsellor is aware that Gerry
has avoided exploring what she has said. She follows his lead and
challenges by repeating what he says.*]

Counsellor: Telling Anna what you want is pressurising her.

Gerry: Of course it is!

Counsellor: I think being part of a couple means joint decision making.
It seems that you have a different view. [*Counsellor challenges
Gerry's perspective by disclosing her view.*]

Gerry: Not really. I'd like us to decide things together, particularly
about our social life, but I don't want to come on all heavy and start
thumping the table. That wouldn't help, would it?

Counsellor: I wonder if you could say what you want without being
angry and thumping the table.

Gerry: [*smiling*] I mean that I want her to take me seriously. That's all.

The counsellor points out to Gerry that the behaviour he has most
control over is his own. He may influence Anna to listen to him and
to do what he wants by the way he responds to her. She continues:

Counsellor: I'm happy to explore some ways of telling Anna what you
want and how you feel. [*The counsellor is concerned to separate goals
from action. Gerry's decision to ask Anna not to go away without him
(goal) needs separating from how he will actually ask her (action).
See Chapter 5.*]

Gerry says that he does not want to pressurise Anna, because he
thinks she will leave him. He says that on one occasion, early on in
their relationship, when he was away, Anna slept with another man.
He feels anxious that Anna will be unfaithful to him over the
weekend. He believes that saying what he wants will give others
power over him. He said that, when he was little, he was told that
asking was rude and he must wait until he was offered. Gerry said
that he was frightened of asking for what he wanted. The counsellor
encouraged him to be concrete about what he believes will happen.
Once Gerry has shared his beliefs, they are then open to exploration
and modification.

Gerry: Oh! that people think I'm not worth considering. Knowing what
I want gives them a chance to stop me from getting it.

Counsellor: I'm not sure who has called you 'worthless' and stopped you
from getting what you want.

Gerry: Well! No one. That's because I'm careful not to ask.

Counsellor: You haven't tested that belief out. [*Challenges by pointing
to a discrepancy.*]

Gerry: If I ask Anna not to go away this weekend, she'll only refuse.
And if I ask her not to sleep with anyone she meets, then she'll say
that I'm being suspicious and it's her life . . .

Counsellor: [*aware that Gerry has not responded to her previous statement*] Gerry, how do you know this?

Gerry: I don't *know*, but it could happen.

Counsellor: You're right, it could happen. You seem to be treating what could happen as what definitely will happen. Make any sense to you?

Gerry: Yes, it does and I suppose, if I don't say anything to her, I'll regret it and feel resentful. If I do ask her not to go, I risk rejection.

Counsellor: I think building relationships and opening ourselves to others does carry risks. Are you willing to take some risks with Anna?

The counsellor points out that being refused a request does not make him a worthless person. Gerry says he would like to tell Anna how he feels and what he wants from her. That is his goal. She reminds him that they are concerned with his behaviour and how he can communicate himself accurately. The following section focussed on action planning (see Chapter 5).

Counsellor: If you imagine yourself talking to Anna, what are you saying?

Gerry: Um! I'll talk to her when she gets home tonight. I'll say what I've said to you. I don't know, something like 'It's inconsiderate accepting invitations without me. I thought this was supposed to be a partnership. I'd rather you didn't go.'

Counsellor: Gerry, you sounded angry and blaming. I wonder if you could think of a way of telling Anna how you feel and what you want without labelling her as inconsiderate.

The counsellor encourages Gerry to label his feelings, to begin by saying 'I feel' and to continue by stating clearly what he wants. Gerry rehearses this several times and gets some feedback from the counsellor. They also discuss when he might talk to Anna and how he will deal with a refusal from her.

Gerry: What if she says 'No! I'm still going.'

Counsellor: I guess that is a possibility. What do you imagine you'll think and feel?

Gerry: I don't know, I'd be angry and disappointed.

Counsellor: And you'd tell yourself?

Gerry: Well! I'd live with it. I wouldn't like it but as you said, I can't make her do what I want. I suppose I'm thinking that, if she doesn't listen to me and consider what I want, then maybe she isn't as committed to me as I want her to be.

Counsellor: Maybe you both want different things from the relationship.

Gerry: And that doesn't make me wrong or worthless!

The session ends with the counsellor recognising that whether or not Gerry stays in his relationship is something she would be willing to explore with him. She also recommends a book about assertive behaviour which he might find useful.

The counsellor reflected on the session. The distinction which she had offered between refusing a request and labelling the person seemed to be a new and liberating perspective for Gerry. He realised that, if Anna refused to do what he wanted, it did not mean he was worthless. He enjoyed the role-play and took the feedback she offered well. In this session, Gerry had moved from exploration through to goal setting and action planning. She was also aware that in the next session she would need to raise the possibility of ending. The initial contract was for six sessions.

Session 5

Gerry arrived looking pensive. He was silent for some minutes. The counsellor decided to wait, because he looked as though he needed time to think.

> *Gerry*: I don't know where to start really. I've had quite a week. I suppose you'd like to know how I got on with Anna.
>
> *Counsellor*: I'm interested to know what happened between you. I'm not sure if you want to begin with that.
>
> *Gerry*: I said what I'd agreed here and she was quite surprised I think. I got angry with her when she refused to give up the weekend. She went on her own but she offered to come back at lunch time on Sunday, so that we could have the afternoon and evening together. I felt pleased about that and we had a relaxed time. I've thought about how I learned not to ask for things and my belief that I won't get them. I caught myself this week thinking that I wouldn't look for a job that I really wanted, because I wouldn't get it. [*Gerry sighed and shrugged his shoulders.*]
>
> *Counsellor*: I think you've made an important connection. One of the ways you stop yourself from having a better work life, is to tell yourself that you won't get what you want. I hope you won't let that belief stop you.
>
> *Gerry*: It's too big a task to tackle. I feel like I've just learned to swim and you're pushing me off the top board. All the jobs I see I'm not qualified for and all the ones I am suitable for I don't want.
>
> *Counsellor*: You think I'm pushing you to move quicker than you want to, is that it? I'm pleased you let me know, I don't want to do that and you don't have to rush. [*Counsellor accepts Gerry's feedback.*]

Gerry says he has been feeling pressurised and that the thought of deciding what changes he wanted and implementing them over the next two weeks seems daunting. The counsellor agrees that making a major change like a career change is likely to take much longer. She reminds Gerry of their initial contract, which was for six sessions with a review and the possibility of further sessions, if he wanted them. She also pointed out that he may finish without having secured another job but with some concrete plans for the future and the confidence to implement them. He decides he would like to opt for a further four sessions. He says that he is feeling more confident about taking responsibility for himself and his future. He would like the support of further sessions while he tackles the issue of changing his job. He continues to talk about work, comparing himself with friends, envying their financial security and the interest they have in what they do. He says he realises that the pressure he experiences is related to fear of being trapped in 'crummy jobs'. The counsellor notices that he is sounding despondent and invites him to say what he is thinking. In the following section, the counsellor's challenges help Gerry to identify and to face his beliefs about himself.

> *Gerry*: [*pauses*] I suppose I have to take what I can get, don't I?
>
> *Counsellor*: I think you can decide what you want and plan to achieve it.
>
> *Gerry*: When you say that, I feel really angry. I can't just take anything I want.
>
> *Counsellor*: Put some words to your anger, Gerry. [*Counsellor gives a directive.*]
>
> *Gerry*: It's hard changing jobs. Interviews are difficult. I won't be able to convince people that I'm serious about changing. They'll find out that I'm a failure. No one will want me.
>
> *Counsellor*: You sound frightened of what you might discover about yourself. Is that it?
>
> *Gerry*: It's what others will discover about me, and I suppose you're right, it's what I'll have confirmed about myself. That I'm a 'no hoper', and that I'll fail. I'll make efforts and have to face the fact that I'm a dead loss. There, I've said it now.
>
> *Counsellor*: And I feel?
>
> *Gerry*: [*slowly*] Relieved, sad too. I guess I don't have a very good opinion of myself.
>
> *Counsellor*: And taking the risk of planning a more demanding job or a training course might confirm your worst fears, that however hard you try you'll never be anything more than a 'no hoper'.

The counsellor decides to challenge Gerry by giving him some feedback on how she sees him. She tells him that she appreciates the way he has talked about himself and she has noticed he has become more open and willing to take risks. She reminds him verbatim of the strengths he identified during the first session and tells him that she believes he can change. She continues by asking him if, in any of his previous interviews, he has ever failed to answer questions well or been called stupid. He admits that this has never happened, rather it is what he fears. He raises his failure at A level again. The counsellor decides to challenge him assertively. She thinks he is hanging on to the past as a way of avoiding risking a different future.

> *Counsellor*: Gerry, I can understand your regret at failing your exam. It seems to me that you're letting that episode blight your life. You don't have to allow that to happen.

> *Gerry*: [*angrily*] 'That's not true!'
> *Counsellor*: I'm way off the mark then.

Gerry is silent for some minutes. He then replies in a flat voice.

> *Gerry*: I guess you're right. That failure seems to loom large, like a huge brick wall, which I can't climb over. It's like I had potential which I wasted.
> *Counsellor*: Potential is a limited commodity, is it? Once you've failed to use it, it's all gone?
> *Gerry*: [*laughing*] That sounds absurd!

Gerry has returned to the theme of failure. Each time he explores what he sees as his failures – at school and subsequently at work – he begins to articulate beliefs that he has about himself, other people and what will happen in his life. He is gradually unhooking from and beginning to question his assessment of himself and his future. In the following dialogue, the counsellor invites Gerry to explore his fantasies of success and failure. He reveals that he has what he calls 'flights of fancy' in which he imagines himself successful at work, married to Anna and they have children.

> *Counsellor*: In your fantasy what usually happens?
> *Gerry*: It ends in misery and disaster. You know, like getting the sack suddenly or Anna announcing unexpectedly that she's going to leave me. I'm usually arriving home from work. [*stops and thinks*] I find a letter from Anna, telling me that she's left and isn't coming back. I feel devastated. It's as if this is what I've been waiting for. It's difficult to explain but it's like I knew that my worst fears were being realised.
> *Counsellor*: And then?
> *Gerry*: I feel wretched and depressed and hopeless. And – well nothing – I get on with my life as best I can.
> *Counsellor*: So you feel very sad and frightened. In spite of intense feelings and believing that you're hopeless, you get on with life. Am I understanding you?
> *Gerry*: I'm frightened of feeling so bad and I want to run away from sadness. I do cope though.
> *Counsellor*: I wonder how you feel hearing yourself say that.
> *Gerry*: I feel like a weight has been lifted off my shoulders. The worst that could happen is that I'll be very sad and I'll cope. I'd really hate it but I'd get through.

The counsellor suggest that Gerry now construct a positive future scenario which he might translate into some concrete goals (see Chapter 5). She asks him to imagine himself five years into the future and talks from that point in time.

The session ends with the counsellor and Gerry reviewing the work. Gerry has shared some painful fantasies and explored some positive scenarios. He also began to realise that fantasising something – good or bad – will not necessarily make it happen; and that he had used his expectation of catastrophe to limit himself and stop himself from acting effectively. The counsellor also challenged Gerry by pointing out that someone calling him a failure or stupid does not mean that is what he is; and that misery does not inevitably follow success. (Chapter 4 refers to aspects of client behaviour that a counsellor might challenge.) In this session, Gerry's counsellor helped him to identify his beliefs about himself and the world. He began to understand more clearly how he restricted himself.

Session 6

Session 6 begins in the following manner:

> *Gerry*: I've been thinking about myself and decided that I'm unfit. I think I'll take more exercise. I used to play badminton, but I've stopped. Anna doesn't play and so I sort of stopped going. That's my plan for the next few months.
>
> *Counsellor*: Get into better physical shape, eh?
>
> *Gerry*: [*in a slow and aimless way*] Yes! I thought I'd take up squash too. I've played once or twice and liked it. It's supposed to be easy to become good enough to enjoy and hard exercise. I used to be good at sport at school, and athletics.

The session continues with several more interchanges in which Gerry talks in a desultory way about what he's going to do to pick up his 'old life' again.

> *Counsellor*: Gerry, I'm not sure that we're talking about what's important for you.
>
> *Gerry*: [*silent for a couple of minutes*] I want to continue talking about changing my job and doing something else but I haven't made much headway.

He said that, after the last session, he felt confident and positive about himself. He intended to fill in an application form he received but has not done so. He imagines himself in interviews justifying or discussing what he has written. He ends by saying that he is bound 'to mess them up'. What follows is the counsellor's invitation to Gerry to be specific about what he imagines he might do.

> *Counsellor*: I'm not sure how you will mess up any interviews you have. [*Counsellor invites Gerry to be concrete.*]
>
> *Gerry*: The way most people do I suppose, mess up the questions.
>
> *Counsellor*: Gerry, I'm interested in how *you* will fail at interviews, which may or may not be what others do.
>
> *Gerry*: It's coping with questions about my past jobs. It's not that I expect them to be difficult but I'll get tongue tied and waffle.

The counsellor prompts Gerry to explore further how he feels and what he thinks when he is asked questions about what he perceives as his lack of achievement. He imagines the interviewers are thinking what a waste of time it is talking to him and how little he has to offer. The counsellor offers to give him some feedback as a way of offering him an alternative perspective on his behaviour. What follows is an example of how the counsellor stays with Gerry after he dismisses her feedback. She invites him to further exploration.

> *Counsellor*: Gerry, I can understand your apprehension about being interviewed. I've experienced you differently in these sessions [*Gerry smiles and nods*], I think you've talked clearly and thoughtfully about yourself. I haven't heard you tongue tied or 'waffle'. I don't think it's a waste of time talking to you.
>
> *Gerry*: Oh! well it's different here. You're not going to give me a job and anyway you're paid to listen to my moaning, aren't you?
>
> *Counsellor*: I'm interested in what happened when I gave you that feedback. You seemed to dismiss it. I wonder what you were thinking and feeling. [*Here the counsellor uses immediacy to focus on the way Gerry has dismissed her feedback to him.*]
>
> *Gerry*: I felt suspicious. I thought you don't mean it and you're just saying that to boost me up.
>
> *Counsellor*: So I was mollifying you. I wonder why I should want to do that! Any ideas? [*Counsellor uses a rhetorical question to encourage Gerry to explore how he dismissed a piece of positive feedback because it did not fit in with his view of himself.*]
>
> *Gerry*: I don't really think you're trying to 'soft soap' me. I suppose that's what I do though. I think people don't mean it when they pay me compliments. I think to myself, they're only saying nice things to be sociable.
>
> *Counsellor*: You ignore comments that contradict your view of yourself. So one of the ways you maintain a negative view of yourself is to disregard positives from others. Does that fit in any way?
>
> *Gerry*: I don't remember much in the way of compliments from others recently. Perhaps I haven't had any or perhaps I've overlooked them. So all this is my fault, is it? My mother always told me I was my own worst enemy.

The counsellor gives Gerry some information about the difference between *recognising* and *blaming*. She reiterates that one of the aims of counselling is to help clients understand how they perceive and process information, so that they can both update their beliefs and substitute more realistic and constructive interpretations. She asks Gerry if he would be willing to record any praise he receives during the following week and share it with her. He agrees to do this.

The counsellor returns to the subject of interviews and checks what Gerry wants to talk about for the rest of the session. Gerry replies that he thinks he will need to brush up on his interview skills, because it is so long since he has had an interview which was important to him or where he thought he would have to sell himself.

> *Counsellor*: That sounds sensible to me. However, I wonder if we are avoiding looking at what specific change you want to make. My hunch is that your lack of enthusiasm over the application forms was partly due to the fact that you don't know where you want to end up. How does that sound to you?
>
> *Gerry*: I guess I don't know exactly what I want. I want some training and I suppose I'll know the right thing for me when I see it. I haven't thought that far ahead. I imagined something turning up! I suppose I feel a bit aimless because I don't know what I'm looking for and . . . [*shrugs his shoulders*].
>
> *Counsellor*: That sounds vague to me. Do you want to find a more specific focus for your search?
>
> *Gerry*: Um! Yes, I suppose so, but what if I choose something I can't have?
>
> *Counsellor*: It seems to me that is what achieving your goals is about, choosing a career that you are able to enter. Part of making that choice will be weighing up options and discovering what is possible and what is not possible. I imagine that you may want to take Anna into account in any decision you make, particularly if you are considering a future together. I also think that some options will carry more risks than others. It will be for you to decide, with help from me if you want, just what risks and costs you are prepared to incur. I suggest that we start with some plans for gaining some information so that you can begin to decide what sort of change you want.

In the above dialogue, the counsellor shares how she sees the goal setting and action planning process. They continue by drawing up a concrete plan of action for gaining information. Gerry agrees to start some research during the week and discuss his findings at his next session. They move on to explore what the job search might mean to Gerry, and the counsellor asks him how he will sustain himself through a period when he may confront the fact that some options are no longer open to him. Gerry dismisses this and says he believes that he has enough stamina to sustain a few knocks. The session ends.

The counsellor reflects on the session and thinks that Gerry may not do what he says he will. His unwillingness to consider how he might sustain himself may mean that he was overlooking the amount of effort and energy needed to implement his goals.

Session 7

Gerry arrives looking sheepish. He announces with a laugh that he has made little progress with either his information search or discussing his ideas with Anna.

Gerry: Well basically, I've done nothing much. I looked in the papers for a few days to get some ideas, but then I lost interest. I wrote down a list of all the options which would interest me. I also looked at the people at work who are doing jobs that I'd like and that's as far as I've got. I met a friend for a drink after I last saw you and he's doing well. I was at school with him and I used to think he was a bit of a plodder, just shows how wrong you can be.

Counsellor: What was on your list? [*Counsellor does not respond to the invitation from Gerry to discuss his friends.*]

Gerry: Most of the jobs needed academic qualifications, like degrees, which I don't have. [*He laughs again.*] Don't laugh but I've drawn up a list of things I can't have. Back to square one.

Counsellor: I'm not laughing. It's not too late for you to get further qualifications now.

Gerry: It would be difficult.

Counsellor: But not impossible! Many people who are older than you decide on higher education.

Gerry: [*sounding interested*] I don't think I could afford it and, anyway, what about Anna?

Counsellor: I wonder if the idea has enough appeal for you to do some research on it?

Gerry: I've always thought the idea was impossible. I feel quite interested. I don't know whether I could afford to give up work or whether Anna will support me though.

Counsellor: I don't know whether you will get a degree. It may be something you decide not to do. However, you're talking about giving up work and there are ways of studying part-time which need not entail that. You also have skills that you could use to make money at weekends and in the holidays, if you wanted the experience of studying full-time. I think you need information about routes and the costs of those routes.

Gerry: You mean financial costs?

Counsellor: Yes, and time and energy too. Part-time studying tends to be spread over a longer period of time. You may not want to study and work full-time. On the other hand, you may prefer that to being without a job.

In the above section, the counsellor uses information to challenge Gerry to consider an option he has been overlooking. Using information to challenge is discussed in Chapter 4.

They continue by exploring one of Gerry's inhibiting beliefs about studying.

Gerry: If you don't study when you leave school, it's too late.

Counsellor: Who told you that?

Gerry: I don't know. I think it was around at school and in my family. I remember my father saying things like that when I left school – 'once you stop, it's harder to get going'. I've always thought it's too late for me.

Counsellor: Your study skills may be rustier now than when you first left school, but that's different from it being too late, isn't it?

Gerry: When I left school, studying was *the* last thing I wanted to do.

The counsellor asks Gerry if he would like to appraise the option of studying full-time for a degree to see whether or not it would be feasible. The method of appraising goals and options for action is discussed in Chapter 5. The counsellor describes the process of brainstorming. She takes a piece of paper and makes two columns, heading them 'Pros' and 'Cons'.

> *Counsellor*: We'll do an analysis by listing all the things that might both help you (pros) and hinder you (cons). From the list, you'll be able to see more clearly whether the goal is feasible and what information you need. What do you think is going on in your life now that will help you and/or hinder you in getting on to a degree course?
>
> *Gerry*: There's Anna. I don't know about her. She may support me and then again she may not.
>
> *Counsellor*: Let's make the list first and evaluate when you think it's complete. [*Discussion may inhibit Gerry from voicing his ideas.*]

Gerry begins to list his ideas as follows:

Pros	*Cons*
– determination	– parents
– ability	– Anna
– current job	– money
– want the opportunity	– scared I'll fail
– will feel better about myself	– purpose – what do I want
– I believe I'm capable	this for?
– earning power – I've always	– age
been able to get work	– forgotten how to study
– adaptable – have	
experienced a range of work	
situations	

The counsellor prompts Gerry to expand his list as follows:

> *Counsellor*: I notice you haven't mentioned friends. I wonder if you know anyone who has done what you are planning to do.
>
> *Gerry*: No, I don't but I've got a couple of friends who had a year off between school and college. They may be helpful to discuss this with. I'll add them to the 'pros' side.

The counsellor encourages Gerry to review his list and identify the major helping and hindering factors. His initial assessment is that he has identified enough that is positive to encourage him to pursue this option further. He identifies money as a major concern and realises that he needs more information. He works with the counsellor to identify both what he needs to find out and how to estimate the maximum amount he will need to live on. He also decides to investigate what financial support is available to mature students.

The counsellor asks him about his parents and Anna, who he sees as the people who are unlikely to support him. Again he says he thinks that they may be against the idea but he is not sure. It is near the end of the session and Gerry decides that it is worth doing costings and discussing the idea with Anna. He agrees to do this by the next session. Before he leaves, the counsellor realises that she has not asked Gerry to share one piece of positive feedback he has received during the week. He tells her with some pleasure that one of the people he works with had told him he was 'bright'.

Session 8

Gerry looks pleased when he comes into the room. He has done some provisional costings and, even though he would be less well off, he thinks he will be able to manage financially. He has not talked to Anna or his parents. He says he has put the conversation off. The counsellor decides to challenge Gerry by posing a hypothetical question:

> *Counsellor*: What's the worst that could happen, when you tell Anna or your parents about your plans?
> *Gerry*: They would both say they don't want to have anything more to do with me.
> *Counsellor*: How likely is that?
> *Gerry*: I don't think my parents would for a moment. They might say 'Don't come running to us, if it all goes wrong', but I've never done that anyway.
> *Counsellor*: And Anna?
> *Gerry*: I don't know. She may not be supportive, if I move to another town and we won't see so much of each other. I'm anxious about that.
> *Counsellor*: When you say you're anxious that Anna won't support you, you're telling me that you're scared about losing her. [*Counsellor focussed on what Gerry is hinting at rather than openly stating.*]
> *Gerry*: Yes, that's about it. She'll say it's either study or me.
> *Counsellor*: And you'll be torn.

They continue by working out how he will tell Anna about his possible plans and how he will respond to an ultimatum, if she gives one. The counsellor reminds him of the work they did in their fourth session about expressing feelings and wants appropriately. They also discuss what sort of relationship he wants and Gerry says again that he does not want a relationship 'at any price'.

They return to the list Gerry made the previous week and begin to look at the positive factors. He says that getting out of his current job would give him an impetus. He believes he has the ability and determination to sustain further study. The counsellor points out that most of the 'pros' relate to feeling more positive about himself, which was the issue that he brought to counselling.

The session ends with Gerry feeling apprehensive about revealing his plans and also excited about the possible changes.

Session 9

At the start of the penultimate session, Gerry looks buoyant as he says he has told his parents that he is thinking of doing a degree course. Far from disapproving, they have been supportive to the extent of offering to help him financially, if he thinks he will need it. He says he was touched by their concern for him and has let go of some of the resentment he has carried towards them. He says that he realises now that they were doing their best for him and he has begun to stop blaming them.

> *Counsellor*: And Anna?
> *Gerry*: Telling her was difficult. She said she didn't expect things to last between us, because couples don't stay together, if they don't see each other much and have different life-styles. It was useful discussing what to say to her last week. I told her, if we wanted to stay together, then we would need to find ways of doing that. I told her the future doesn't have to be like she believes it will be. I don't know what will happen between us.
> *Counsellor*: And you?
> *Gerry*: I'm excited, and I've more or less decided that if I can get a place, I'll go.
> *Counsellor*: You've more or less decided?

Gerry goes on to say he is anxious about making the choice, because he feels that he has not made good decisions in the past. He wants to succeed and to enjoy the experience. The counsellor challenges him by asking him to compare the way he is tackling this decision to the way he has made decisions in the past.

> *Counsellor*: I don't think any decision is risk free. How is making this decision different from the way you have made decisions in the past?
> *Gerry*: I'm planning this one more carefully. I've got a good idea what some of the risks might be. I'm clear about what I'll be doing the course for. I suppose I'm being far more purposeful.
> *Counsellor*: So, you're planning and anticipating in a way that you haven't before?
> *Gerry*: Yes! I don't think I've ever planned like this. I've usually taken what's been offered to me. I don't think I believed I deserved to have what I wanted.

They continue by brainstorming a list of information which will help Gerry to make a decision about which course and which institution. They review the list and discuss what information might be available to him and how he might obtain it. They develop an action plan for gaining and evaluating the information.

> *Counsellor*: Gerry, next week is our last session of the ten we agreed on.
> *Gerry*: I've been thinking about that. I think I'll end. I know I've still got to make the decision about which course, but I've realised that is what I want to do and I know how to make that happen. I've got a plan.
> *Counsellor*: I'd like to suggest that we spend next week reviewing what you've achieved and clearing any unfinished issues you may have with me.

Session 10 – Final Session

Gerry says he has made a decision to return to studying. He has gained some information and thinks he will be able to gain a place on a full-time course. His other options are part-time and distance learning. He has not yet identified where he would like to study, but is clearer about what subject he will choose. He says that he feels more purposeful and more in control of his life. The session is spent reviewing what Gerry thinks he has achieved in counselling and looking to the future.

> *Gerry*: I feel much stronger in myself and I've realised that, while I've felt anxious about taking this step, I haven't felt depressed or bad tempered. My moods were really about being trapped and pushed around, although no one was actually pushing me.
> *Counsellor*: You were trapping yourself with your beliefs about being 'useless' and a failure. You think differently about yourself now.
> *Gerry*: Yes, I know that I can plan and decide what I want. I don't have to sit like a lump, moaning and waiting for others to act.
> *Counsellor*: You can influence what happens to you.
> *Gerry*: Yes, I can. I feel on a firmer footing with Anna too. I used to be frightened of standing up for myself.
> *Counsellor*: Of saying what you wanted in the relationship.
> *Gerry*: Yes! Rather than standing up for myself. That sounds a bit too aggressive. I suspect that I used to hint and wait so much, that any action I took I saw as standing up for myself. I don't feel so scared of the future either. I may not get what I want but I'm going to go for a degree.

Counsellor nods and Gerry continues.

> *Gerry*: Well, I've got a plan now. More than that, I think I've got the energy to make changes and to take risks. I remember the session we had about money. I had always thought full-time study was out of the question and when you recommended I do some costings I was shocked. When I got home, I realised I was cross with you. I thought

you were trying to push me. [*laughing*] I was looking forward to telling you that it was too expensive and out of the question.

Counsellor: You knew what was possible without gaining more information. I wonder if you're still angry with me.

Gerry: I'm not angry now. I realise that I didn't know and I was assuming. While I didn't test the money issue out or have any hard information, I didn't have to face the fact that study might be possible. And I guess that presented me with a choice which I didn't think I had.

Counsellor: And a choice that was and I guess still is risky for you.

Gerry: Yes, it is, because when we looked at my information wants last week and I wrote 'to know that I'll succeed', I realised that life is uncertain and no one can give me that information.

The counsellor is impressed with the way Gerry is talking about how he sees himself and what he has gained. She gives him some feedback about how he presents himself now compared with how she first experienced him.

Counsellor: I can see a change in you. You're talking in a more purposeful way. You seem to value yourself much more and recognise that you have abilities and strengths. When we first met, you didn't believe you deserved to get what you wanted. Is that right?

Gerry: Yes, I was really pathetic!

Counsellor: I didn't see you as pathetic and I don't think it's helpful to label yourself so negatively. You were struggling to change aspects of your life and your beliefs about yourself when you came here. That's not a weak thing to do.

Gerry: I know. I'm joking, because I'm sad I'm finishing in one way and, in another, I'm pleased I've got a sense of direction.

Counsellor: I shall miss seeing you. I can understand that you feel sad that we won't be meeting again. I'm pleased that you feel positive about the future.

Gerry talks about other times he has lost touch with people. He says that in his past he has experienced unhappy endings, rejecting before he was rejected.

Counsellor: What's different about this ending for you?

Gerry: Well, I don't feel angry or threatened. I suppose I feel like I'm riding my bike without the stabilisers! I've been thinking over the past week about leaving school and leaving my various jobs. The overriding urge I've had is wanting to get away from. I want to get on with sorting out my plan for the future, but I don't think I'm running away.

Counsellor: I don't think you're running away. I think you're looking forwards and that seems very different to me.

Gerry: And to me!

The counsellor mentions that they have fifteen minutes left and asks Gerry if there is anything on his mind. For example, if he has left-over feelings from any previous sessions that he wants to express and clear.

> *Gerry*: I don't think so. The session which sticks in my mind is the one where I was angry with you. I imagined that, when I came in the next week, you'd tell me to 'clear off'.
>
> *Counsellor*: Showing anger when you were young was a punishable offence, was it?
>
> *Gerry*: Yes, it was rude and therefore not allowed. It was quite a surprise when you didn't tell me to mind my manners. Well, in one sense it was a surprise and in another I guess I was testing you.
>
> *Counsellor*: What do you think you took away from that session, then?
>
> *Gerry*: That feelings aren't bad or rude. And I can say what I feel without blaming or being unpleasant. I also have the choice of when and whether to say what I think and feel.

The session ends with the counsellor wishing Gerry well. He asks if she will be willing to see him again in the future, if he wants further counselling. The counsellor has a hunch that Gerry wants both to soften the ending for himself and to keep his options for further support open, if he thinks he will want it. She also wonders whether he wants to give her a 'progress report' by letting her know how he is faring. She replies

> *Counsellor*: Yes, of course and I'll fit you in as soon as possible, if you decide to contact me in the future.

She decides not to invite him to let her know how he is getting on in the future. She thinks this will blur the ending of what has been a contractual counselling relationship.

Postscript

The counsellor reviews her work with Gerry. She thinks that he has a more positive and realistic view of himself. He has become more purposeful in shaping his life as a result of his altered self-perception. He left counselling without implementing the job change he wanted. This is a long-term aim, dependent upon Gerry achieving his short-term goals of both entering higher education and succeeding in getting a degree. He used the sessions well to deal with particular issues which were concerning him. The central theme of the sessions was Gerry's view of himself and, while his self-esteem has grown, the counsellor believes he may seek further counselling help, particularly over relationship issues. Her impression of Gerry is that he has done enough work for the present to change the direction of his life.

References

Argyle, M. (1988) *Bodily Communication*, 2nd edn. London: Methuen.

Benjamin, A. (1974) *The Helping Interview*, 2nd edn. Boston: Houghton Mifflin.

Bond, T. (1989) 'Towards defining the role of counselling skills', *Counselling: The Journal of the British Association for Counselling*, 69: 3–9.

Brammer, L., Shostrom, E. and Abrego, P. (1988) *Therapeutic Psychology: Fundamentals of Counseling and Psychotherapy*, 5th edn. Engelwood Cliffs, NJ: Prentice-Hall.

Brammer, L.M. (1988) *The Helping Relationship: Processes and Skills*, 4th edn. Englewood Cliffs, NJ: Prentice-Hall.

British Association for Counselling (1984) *Code of Ethics and Practice for Counsellors*, Form No. 14.

Dainow, S. and Bailey, C. (1988) *Developing Skills with People: Training for Person to Person Client Contact*. Chichester: Wiley.

d'Ardenne, P. and Mahtani, A. (1989) *Transcultural Counselling in Action*. London: Sage.

Deaux, K. and Wrightsman, L. S. (1984) *Social Psychology in the 80s*, 4th edn. Monterey, Calif.: Brooks/Cole.

Dinnage, R. (1988) *One to One: The Experience of Psychotherapy*. London: Viking.

Dryden, W. (1990) *Rational-Emotive Counselling in Action*. London: Sage.

Egan, G. (1977) *You and Me*. Monterey, CA.: Brooks/Cole.

Egan, G. (1985) *Exercises in Helping Skills*, 3rd edn. Monterey, CA.: Brooks/Cole.

Egan, G. (1986) *The Skilled Helper: A Systematic Approach to Effective Helping*, 3rd edn. Monterey, Calif.: Brooks/Cole.

Ellis, A. (1962) *Reason and Emotion in Psychotherapy*. New York: Lyle Stuart.

Gilmore, S.K. (1973) *The Counselor-in-Training*. Englewood Cliffs, NJ: Prentice-Hall.

Gilmore, S.K. and Fraleigh, P.W. (1980) *Communication at Work*. Eugene, OR: Friendly Press.

Hawkins, P. and Shohet, R. (1989) *Supervision in the Helping Professions*. Milton Keynes: Open University Press.

Hobson, R.F. (1985) *Forms of Feeling: The Heart of Psychotherapy*. London: Tavistock.

Hopson, B. and Scally, M. (1982) *Life Skills Teaching Programmes*, No. 2. Leeds: Life Skills Associates.

Ivey, A.E., Ivey, M.B. and Simek-Downing, L. (1987) *Counseling and Psychotherapy: Integrating Skills, Theory and Practice*, 2nd edn. Englewood Cliffs, NJ: Prentice-Hall.

Jacobs, M. (1985) *Swift to Hear*. London: SPCK.

Lewin, K. (1969) 'Quasi-stationary social equilibria and the problem of permanent change', in W.G. Bennis, K.D. Benne and R. Chin (eds), *The Planning of Change*. New York: Holt, Rinehart and Winston.

Marx, R. (1984) 'Self control strategies in management training', paper given at American Psychological Association meeting, Toronto, Canada, August.

Mearns, D. and Dryden, W. (1989) *Experiences of Counselling in Action*. London: Sage.

Mearns, D. and Thorne, B. (1988) *Person-Centred Counselling in Action*. London: Sage.

Mickelson, D. and Stevic, R. (1971) 'Differential effects of facilitative and non-facilitative behavioural counsels', *Journal of Counselling Psychology*, 18: 314–19.

Munro, A., Manthei, B. and Small, J. (1989) *Counselling: The Skills of Problem Solving*. London: Routledge.

Nelson-Jones, R. (1988) *Practical Counselling and Helping Skills*, 2nd edn. London: Cassell.

Nelson-Jones, R. (1989) *Effective Thinking Skills: Preventing and Managing Personal Problems*. London: Cassell.

Oldfield, S. (1983) *The Counselling Relationship: A Study of the Client's Experience*. London: Routledge and Kegan Paul.

Reddy, M. (1987) *The Manager's Guide to Counselling at Work*. London: Methuen.

Rogers, C. (1951) *Client Centred Therapy: Its Current Practice, Implications and Theory*. Boston: Houghton Mifflin.

Rogers, C. (1961) *On Becoming a Person*. London: Constable.

Rowan, J. (1983) *The Reality Game: A Guide to Humanistic Counselling and Therapy*. London: Routledge and Kegan Paul.

Steiner, C. (1984) 'Emotional literacy', *Transactional Analysis Journal*, 14 (3): 162–73.

Storr, A. (1980) *The Art of Psychotherapy*. New York: Methuen.

Strong, S. (1968) 'Counseling: an interpersonal influence process', *Journal of Counseling Psychology*, 15: 215–24.

Sugarman, L. (1986) *Life Span Development: Concepts, Theories and Interventions*. London: Methuen.

Trower, P., Casey, A. and Dryden, W. (1988) *Cognitive-Behavioural Counselling in Action*. London: Sage.

Truax, C.B. and Carkhuff, R.R. (1967) *Toward Effective Counseling and Psychotherapy*. Chicago: Aldine.

Tyler, L.E. (1969) *The Work of the Counselor*, 3rd edn. New York: Appleton Century Crofts.

Ward, D.E. (1984) 'Termination of individual counseling: concepts and strategies', *Journal of Counseling and Development*, 63: 21–5; in W. Dryden (ed.), *Key Issues in Counselling in Action*. London: Sage, 1989.

Watzlawick, P., Weakland, J. and Fisch, R. (1974) *Change: Principles of Problem Formation and Problem Resolution*. London: Norton.

Index

acceptance by counsellor 4, 9, 12–13, 22, 41, 42–3
advice v. information 82
aims
    of beginning 3–4, 11–18
    of ending 7, 91–3
    of middle 6, 62–4
    see also goals
anger 37, 44, 45, 71, 72, 78, 142
anxiety 24, 28, 86–7, 101–2
approach to counselling, counsellor's explanation of 26
assessments by counsellor 3, 12, 15–17, 30
assumptions about human nature 9–10
attending 4, 35–8

balance-sheet
    of outcomes 96
    of resources/constraints 104, 137
beginning stage of counselling 3–5, 11–34
    aims of 3–4, 11–18
    first session 22–34, 116–21
    skills of 4–5
    strategies of 4, 18–22
behaviour
    and goals 99
    consequences of 69–70
    purposeful nature of 10
beliefs, faulty 70, 71, 76–7, 126
bereavement 81
blaming
    avoiding 73, 81
    of others 78
    of self 79
'blind spots' 66
boundary issues 88–9
brainstorming 101–3, 137

case-study 116–42
challenging 6–7, 14, 64–89
    aims of 71

as deeper exploration 66–9
confrontation as 75–80
counsellor's openness to 73–4
encouraging self-challenge 73, 79
giving directives as 82–4
giving feedback as 80–1
giving information as 81–2
how to challenge 71–5
immediacy in 86–9, 125–6
in goal setting 100
self-disclosure by counsellor as 84–6
skill sequence for 74–5
types of challenge 75–89
what to challenge 69–71
change
    deciding on 7, 91, 93–107
    implementing 7, 91–2, 107–12
    obstacles to 109–10
    planning 8, 107–9
    possibility of 9
    sustaining 110–12
childhood experiences 94, 124–5, 127
choice point, forming 47
clarifying 29, 45–6
classifying information from clients 16, 38–9, 121
closed questions 51–2
closeness/distance, emotional 14
closure of sessions 46
    first session 33–4
communication skills 1
    non-verbal 35–6, 67
    probing 5, 49–59
    reflective 4–5, 41–9
concrete, being 5, 59–60, 72–3, 80–1
confidentiality 32
confrontation 6, 75–80
connections, making 68–9
consequences of behaviour, lack of understanding of 69–70
constraints on client 20–1
contact with clients, making 23–4
context of client's problems 29

contract, counselling
  negotiating 3–4, 17–18, 30–3
  pursuing work of 64
  renegotiating 6
contrasting 31
control
  by counsellor 55
  emotional 112
core values, communicating 4, 6, 12–13, 22
cultural norms 40

delaying tactics by client 78
depression 117
dimensions of human existence 16, 121
directives, giving 6, 82–4
discrepancies, confronting 69, 77–8
duration of counselling 30

Egan, G. 12, 66, 67
'either/or' questions 52–3
empathy 41, 67
ending stage of counselling 7–8, 90–115
  aims of 7, 91–3
  skills of 8; *see also* skills of
    counselling
  strategies of 7–8, 93–112
  termination of counselling 112–15, 140–2
evaluation
  by client 70, 125–6
  of client's behavioural changes 8, 111
exhaustion problems 68–9
expectations, client's 22–3, 25
exploration 2–3, 4, 18–21, 22, 29, 31
  closing down 55–6
  deeper 66–9
  in goal setting 100
  skill sequence for 58–9
eye contact in counselling 35–6, 38

facial expression 36
failure 131–2
family problems 21, 48, 53, 69–70, 96, 123
fantasies, client's 23, 50
feedback, giving 6, 80–1
feelings, getting in touch with 39, 70–1, 83, 85, 87, 92, 118–19

figure–ground perspective, gaining 47–8
filtering information 40–1
first session 22–34, 116–21
focussing 4, 19–20, 21, 46
forcefield analysis 104–6
foundation skills of counselling *see* skills
  of counselling
frame of reference 41
frequency of sessions 30
futures, imagining 100–1, 132

Gilmore, S.K. 16
goals, 7, 93–107
  and brainstorming 101–3
  and forcefield analysis 104–6
  and identifying options 100–4
  and imagining futures 100–1
  and sentence completion 103–4
  appraisal of 104–6
  assessability of 99
  client's views on 9–10, 31–2, 95–6
  difficulties in setting 106
  suitability of 96–9

hopes, client's 22–3
humour, as a defence 119
hypotheses/hunches, counsellor's 37, 41, 47–8
hypothetical questions 50–1

identity dimension 16, 121
immediacy 7, 86–9, 125–6
implications, focussing on 67
inferences/interpretations, faulty 69, 70
information, giving 6, 81–2
interview problems 80, 131, 133–5
introduction to client 24–9
issues in counsellor's life 40
Ivey, A.E. et al. 36

jargon, avoidance of 26
judgements by counsellor 12
  client's fear of 26–7

labelling client 80
leading questions 53–4
learning
  reviewing 8, 115
  transferring 7, 92
length of sessions 30

'life-space' 104
listening 4, 5, 35, 38–41, 67
    filters in 40–1
    framework for 38–9
    to own reactions 40
    to silences 39–40

meaning, creation of 9
'mental picture' of counsellor, client's 92
meta-model of counselling 8
middle stage of counselling 5–7, 61–89
    aims of 6, 62–4
    challenging strategies for 6–7, 64–5
    skills of 7; *see also* skills of
        counselling
    types of challenge 75–89
moving counselling forward 46
multiple questions 53

negative effects of questions 55–6
negative feedback from clients 114–15
negotiation 17–18, 31–2
Nelson-Jones, R. 70
non-verbal behaviour 67
    client's 36–7, 39–40, 126
    counsellor's 35–6, 37–8, 54
number of sessions 30

observing clients 36–8
obstacles to action 109–10
open questions 49–50
opening sessions 46
oppressive relationships 73
options, identifying 100–4
outcomes
    balance-sheet of 96
    desirability of 95–6
    imagining 100–1
    realism of 97–9
    see also goals
overlooking strengths/deficits 69, 78, 122
overwork problems 20, 68–9, 98–9

paraphrasing 3, 5, 42–5
pattern, establishing 24–5
payment for counselling 31
perspective, counsellor's 72, 125
planning
    action for change 8, 107–9
    termination of counselling 113–14

posture, counsellor's 35
potential, realising 10
'power', counsellor's 32
powerlessness 112
'presenting concerns' 29
prioritising 4, 21–2, 46
probing skills 5, 49–59, 74
problem definition 3, 14–15, 29
process v. content 1–2

questions to clients 49–57
    closed 51–2
    effects of 54–6
    'either/or' 52–3
    guidelines for 54
    hypothetical 50–1
    leading 53–4
    multiple 53
    open 49–50
    unhelpful 51–4
    'Why?' questions 51
questions to counsellor 56–7, 120

rationalising 78
reactions, counsellor's 40
realism of goals 97–9
reassessment of problems 6, 62–3
referral process 23, 28
reflective skills 4–5, 41–9, 74
relationship, client–counsellor 87–9, 94,
   121
    establishing 3, 12–14
    maintaining 6, 63–4
    terminating 7, 92–3, 113–14
relationship dimension 16, 121
relationship problems 27, 50, 52–3, 55,
   57, 73, 81, 92, 97, 98, 116, 118, 121,
   126–30, 138, 139
renegotiation 32
resources *see* strengths/resources
restating 5, 41–2
retirement 95
reviewing counselling work 8, 115
reward system 110–11, 112
risks of change 110
Rogers, C. 12, 13

sadness 27, 39, 93–4, 113–14
seating arrangements in counselling 36
self-challenge, encouraging 73, 79

self-disclosure
  by client 20
  by counsellor 6–7, 84–6
self-esteem, low 39–40, 42, 43–4, 72–3,
  108, 118–19, 120, 123, 131
sentence completion 103
silences 39–40
skill deficits 106, 109–10
skills of counselling 3, 35–60
  attending 4, 35–8
  being concrete 5, 59–60
  listening 4, 38–41
  of beginning stage 4–5
  of ending stage 8
  of middle stage 7
  probing skills 5, 49–59
  reflective skills 4–5, 41–9
social life, improving 98–9, 103, 106
specificity, encouraging 19; *see also*
  concrete, being
stages of counselling 2, 8; *see also*
  beginning stage of counselling;
  ending stage of counselling; middle
  stage of counselling
statements by counsellors 5, 57–8
Steiner, C. 85
strategies 2–3
  client's 12–13
  of beginning stage of counselling 4,
  18–22
  of ending stage of counselling 7–8,
  93–112
  of middle stage of counselling 6–7,
  64–89

strengths/resources
  confronting 78–9, 122–3
  overlooking 69, 78
stuckness 88
study problems 104–5, 136–9
summarising 5, 45–9
support
  establishing system for 111
  from counsellor 14
  need for 87–8

tentativeness from counsellor 71
termination of counselling 112–15, 140–2
themes, identifying 67–8
trainee counsellors 81–2
trust, client–counsellor 14, 43, 83–4, 88

understanding by counsellor 4, 9, 13, 22,
  41, 42–3
unexpressed thoughts/feelings, listening
  for 67, 70–1

vagueness 19, 58, 59, 96
values
  client's 95–6
  counsellor's 40
vulnerability, client's 72

weight problems 108–9
'Why?' questions 51
work dimension 16, 121
work problems 49, 60, 65–6, 67, 76–7,
  78–9, 84–5, 86–7, 96, 98, 101, 122,
  124, 130–1

Index compiled by Peva Keane